SEALS

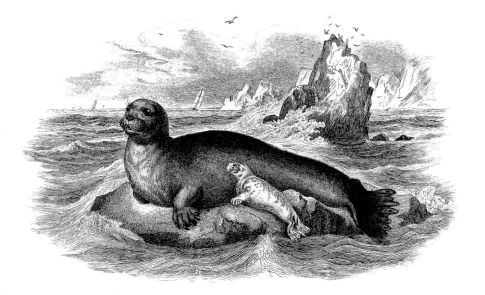

SARA GODWIN

MALLARD PRESS

An Imprint of BDD Promotional Book Company, Inc.
666 Fifth Avenue
New York, NY 10103

A FRIEDMAN GROUP BOOK

Published by MALLARD PRESS
An imprint of BDD Promotional Book Company, Inc.
666 Fifth Avenue
New York, New York 10103

Mallard Press and its accompanying design and logo are trademarks
of BDD Promotional Book Company, Inc.

ISBN 0-792-45258-5

SEALS
was prepared and produced by
Michael Friedman Publishing Group, Inc.
15 West 26th Street
New York, New York 10010

Editor: Melissa Schwarz
Art Director: Robert W. Kosturko
Designer: Deborah Kaplan
Photography Editor: Christopher Bain
Production: Karen L. Greenberg

Typeset by BPE Graphics
Color separations by Universal Colour Scanning, Ltd.
Printed and bound in Hong Kong by Leefung-Asco Printers, Ltd.

DEDICATION

To C.J.,
whom I have loved for the better part
—no, the best part—of my life,
and to Jane and Josh,
who early on decided to let me grow up
to be anything I wanted to be.

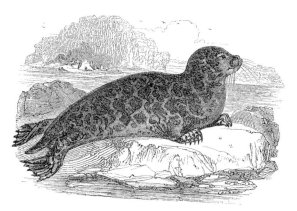

ACKNOWLEDGMENTS

I must extend my grateful thanks to John McCosker, Director, Steinhardt Aquarium, California Academy of Sciences, San Francisco, California, who always made time in his impossible schedule to answer my questions or find me the person who could; to Bill Rohrs, Senior Aquarist at Steinhardt Aquarium, who put at my disposal his knowledge of seals gleaned over 25 years of working with them and let me come play with the seals at the Aquarium; to Steve Bailey, who made the libraries of the California Academy of Sciences available to me for research; to Brian Davies of the International Animal Welfare Fund, who saved the harp seals for me to see; to Jim Norwood of Tourism Canada, who made possible my trip to visit the enchanting baby harp seals of the Magdalen Islands, Canada; to Burney LeBoeuf of the University of California, Santa Cruz, who authorized my visit to Ano Nuevo Island to observe the Northern elephant seals; to Mary Jane Schramm of the California Marine Mammal Rescue Center, Sausalito, California who spent hours showing me every detail of the Rescue Center's operations and taught me the revolting recipe of whipped cream, frozen herring, and vitamin formula the poor little creatures are fed until they can be released back into the wild to feast on some decent raw eel and squid; to Judith King of the University of New South Wales, Australia, without whose painstaking scholarship this book could not have been written; and to Charles James, who ran to ground every lead, miraculously located the books I couldn't find, and turned up grinning with every old *National Geographic* that ever even mentioned seals. This book is a tribute to their knowledge and generosity. Any errors, God forbid, are exclusively my own.

CONTENTS

Chapter One

Pinnipeds: The Finfooted Tribe

Seals are found in every sea in the world and along every coast of every continent. They have many of the qualities that we look for in friends: they are intelligent, curious, amusing, and often well traveled. They are found in the coldest waters of the world, in both the Arctic and the Antarctic, and in some of the warmest, around Hawaii. While many species have been threatened with extinction, today nearly all the endangered species are making a strong comeback. Scientists even hold out hope that the only species believed to be extinct, the West Indian monk seal, may yet exist on some uninhabited Caribbean island.

There are thirty-five species of seals—nineteen true seals (*Phocidae*), fifteen eared seals, which include fur seals and sea lions (*Otariidae*), and the walrus, which has no external ears and a family of its own (*Odobenidae*). Seals are classified primarily on the basis of whether or not their ears are visible, which

Australian sea lion males (far left) aggressively herd females into their territories, and defend their cows just as aggressively. The male rearing up behind the cows is warning an intruder to back off.

Harbor seals (above) are found on all coasts of the Northern Hemisphere, and have been known to swim up rivers that debouch into the ocean. They often perch on sandbars and rocks at low tide and wait for the next high tide to take them back out to the sea.

Both male and female walrus have tusks, as this cow (right) amply demonstrates. The tusks are used as arms to help the walrus hoist itself from the water onto ice floes or up rocks on land, and they are also used most effectively in self-defense.

seems a charming, if whimsical, way of going about things, but no odder than distinguishing plants by the details of their reproductive systems, as Linnaeus—the founder of scientific nomenclature, the father of taxonomy, and the inventor of the Latin binomial—did.

Even on eared seals, the ears aren't much to look at. California sea lions have ears that are about 2½ inches (6 cm) long and are shaped like slim, brown scrolls. Seals without external ears have only a small oval hole no more than ½ inch (1 cm) long which closes completely underwater. Seals hear in air about as well as people, but their hearing underwater is much better and their ability to tell what direction a sound comes from is especially keen. There is considerable evidence that seals, like whales and porpoises, use sonar both to find fish and to avoid obstacles. It is known that seals use sounds that "ping" or bounce back off solid objects, just as dolphins and bats do, but anatomists are baffled that seals' brains do not have the highly developed temporal lobes, used in acoustic analysis, that are found in dolphins, a species famous for its sonar navigation. California sea lions, the ball-balancing seals of circus fame, can find food in total darkness. Sea lions actually find fish faster in total darkness than they do in good light. In

Seasons of the Seal, Fred Bruemmer tells of a blind, but otherwise healthy, gray seal that migrated thousands of miles year after year, returning each year to pup and mate in precisely the same spot, a quarter of a mile inland on Sable Island in the North Atlantic. Scientists speculate that seals use their ears, their eyes, and their whiskers to sense both prey and predators.

If a seal's ears provide its sonar, its whiskers provide the radar. The exact function of the whiskers has not been determined precisely. It is clear, however, that the seal's whiskers act as acutely sensitive antennae, allowing it to feel the underwater vibrations of even the tiniest fish or crustacean.

Seals' whiskers grow in straight lines along the sides of the muzzle, rather like an untidy mustache. Leopard and Ross seals, two southern phocid species, have from fifteen to twenty whiskers on each side of their snouts; most eared seals have from twenty to thirty; southern elephant seals have about thirty-eight; northern phocids, including harbor seals and harp seals, have between forty and fifty; and the walrus sports a luxurious and magnificent mustache with about three hundred whiskers on each side. The walrus's whiskers are the shortest and thickest, only about 3½ inches (8–9 cm) long, while fur seals have the long-

Taking a break from sunbathing on a California beach, this Pacific harbor seal demonstrates that when you've got an itch, you've got to scratch. Harbor seals use both their foreflippers simultaneously to move on land, leaving clear flipper prints in the sand. In the water, the foreflippers are used to change direction, and are streamlined tight against the body when swimming fast.

est. The longest whisker on record, belonging to an Antartic fur seal bull, measured nearly 20 inches (48 cm) in length.

While all seals use their whiskers as tactile organs to examine a new environment or investigate a new neighbor, walruses also use theirs as an emotional barometer, expressing curiosity, amiability, or displeasure with a series of eloquent twitches.

Seals' eyes are adapted to see both in air and underwater. The eyeball itself is unusually large for the animal's size. An elephant seal's eye, the largest among seals, is slightly over 3 inches (7½ cm) in diameter, about the size of a baseball. The eye of a California sea lion is essentially the same size as that of a domestic ox or a Greenland right (bowhead) whale. To give some idea of what this means in terms of the relative size of the animals, California sea lions weigh at most 660 pounds (299 kg), an ox averages 1,100 pounds (499 kg), and a Greenland right whale 100 tons, or *2 million pounds* (1.8 metric tons).

Seals' eyes, like those of cats and other nocturnal predators, are designed for low-light hunting. The pupils, which are scarcely more than vertical slits on land, dilate until they are almost perfectly circular underwater. The *tapetum lucidum*, a silvery layer behind the retina, amplifies all available light like the reflector on a flashlight. The cornea is especially adapted to see underwater, unlike human eyes, which are adapted to seeing in air, becoming blurred underwater. Like most animals other than humans, seals don't really see colors, but their eyes are particularly sensitive to green wavelengths, a useful adaptation for living underwater since sea water tends to be green.

Seals' eyes are protected by upper and lower eyelids, like other mammals, and by a third eyelid called the nictitating membrane, which works like a windshield wiper, wiping the eye of sand and other small particles.

Many of the old sealers reported seeing seals cry, particularly in situations that would cause grief in humans. Brian Davies, founder of the International Animal Welfare Fund, writes in his book *Savage Luxury,* "The pup was skinned alive. I saw the heart, in a body without skin, beating frantically. After the hunter had left the ice, I saw the mother seal crawl back to the shattered carcass of her pup. Great tears flowed from her eyes." Very little is known about emotions in animals, however, and it has not been scientifically proven that seals cry tears of grief. They may merely lubricate the eye.

Like the ears, the nostrils of seals seal tightly when the animals dive. The nostrils also close automatically during sleep, a useful feature in animals that sleep just below the surface of the sea. Seals do not breathe while sleeping underwater. They surface to breathe, often without waking, every ten to fifteen minutes for young seals, every thirty minutes for adults.

Mother seals are believed to recognize their pups largely by smell, and males may use smell to determine if a cow is ready to breed. Despite the fact that seals' olfactory lobes, which provide the sense of smell, are

quite small, Southern sea lions will panic at the scent of a person over 200 yards (183 m) away.

Seals' tongues have few taste buds, and the tongue itself is rather short, but since seals swallow most of their food whole and tend to eat on the run, as it were, there is little occasion for the kind of savoring that taste buds enhance.

Seals tend to be long-lived, surviving up to forty-one years in captivity and forty-six years in the wild. The age of a seal can be determined by counting the concentric rings of its teeth, exactly as the rings of tree trunks are counted to discover the age of a tree. Just as the width of the rings of a tree may indicate the amount of rainfall in a given year, so the rings on the canines of seals indicate periods of fasting, pregnancy, pupping, molting, and even sexual activity.

The food seals eat varies with the species of seal and with the food available in the feeding grounds. In general, seals eat primarily squid, tiny shrimps, krill, shellfish, and fish.

Seals also eat stones, and as much as 24 pounds (11 kg) of small rocks have been found in their stomachs. Even very young

This Antarctic fur seal appears to be having a belligerently confrontational conversation with a chinstrap penguin. Perhaps the dispute is over the astonishing proliferation of Antarctic fur seals, the greatest comeback from the devastation wrought by sealers of all the pinniped species. Does more fur seals mean less room for the chinstrap penguins with which they share their range?

California sea lions climb up slippery rocks in the wild with the same dexterity they use to climb ladders and sit on stools in circuses. On Ano Nuevo Island, in California, sea lions broke into an abandoned lightkeeper's house, galumphed through the back parlor, and climbed the stairs to the upstairs bathroom where one was found reclining in the clawfoot tub.

pups have rocks in their stomachs, baby seals being no different from baby people in their definition of edible, which is, anything that fits in their mouth. This rock-eating phenomenon baffled geologists, as well as biologists, for years. The geologists were seriously disconcerted to find piles of basalt stones on certain Antarctic islands where all the rocks were granite. The explanation, they finally discovered, is that Hooker's sea lions had migrated from the Auckland Islands, which are basalt, and thrown up the rocks they'd eaten on the Snares, where the stone is granite.

No one has the slightest idea why seals eat stones. A number of theories have been advanced, but none are supported by evidence. Some scientists suggest that the stones may help grind up food that is swallowed whole; others think they may crush parasitic worms in the seal's stomach. Perhaps they help the seal regurgitate fish bones, but not all seals throw up their fish bones. Perhaps the stones are for ballast. Perhaps they are eaten to allay hunger pangs when the seals are fasting during breeding and molting. Precisely why seals eat rocks is yet another seal mystery on its way to becoming a doctoral dissertation.

Seals fast for long periods, from two to four months of the year depending on the species. Northern elephant seals fast for three months during the breeding season

and for another month while molting. Males cannot abandon their territory during the breeding season without risking their chance to breed, and females must remain near their pups to nurse and protect them, so they must go without food.

Seals rarely drink in the wild. They appear to get all the moisture they need from their food. Occasionally, seals suffering from leptospirosis, a liver and kidney disease, have been seen drinking fresh water. Sea water makes seals ill, just as it does people.

Much ink has been spilled over the issue of whether seals eat too many of the fish that people also eat, with seals and fishermen portrayed as bitter natural enemies. While there is no question that human and seal tastes in fish sometimes overlap, careful studies show that the vast majority of seals' food consists of noncommercial species. Researchers have found evidence that, in fact, overfishing may damage the ocean food chain to the point that certain seal species cannot find sufficient food. An official of the Canadian Department of Fisheries and Oceans is quoted in Farley Mowat's *Sea of Slaughter* as stating, "There's no solid proof that seals ever were a major problem. In fact, there's good evidence that, as an integral part of the marine biota, their presence is important to the successful propagation of a number of commercial fish species. Look at it this way: in the nineteenth century,

over twice as much cod was being landed as we can get now, even [using] old-fashioned methods. And there were millions of seals out there then.''

Seals are a superb example of form following function. Their streamlined shape, so clumsily blimplike on land, is as efficient in water as a torpedo. They are perfectly designed to slip through the water swiftly and silently. Nothing protrudes to spoil the smooth line. Eared seals use their foreflippers like oars to scull through the water; they don't use their hind flippers for swimming at all. True seals use their hind flippers to swim and their foreflippers to change direction. Walruses get most of their thrust from their hind flippers but use their foreflippers for greater speed as well as to maneuver.

Not much is known about how fast seals swim in the wild. Sea lions and fur seals are believed to reach top speeds of more than 17 miles (28 km) per hour, and true seals nearly 12 miles (19 km) per hour. Walruses generally cruise at about 3 miles (5 km) per hour, but when escaping a predator they are capable of achieving short bursts of speed up to 19 miles (31 km) per hour.

Seals are an example of what is known in scientific circles as "convergent evolution." As similar as all seals look today, the species are, in fact, descended from two entirely

© John Cancalosi/Tom Stack & Associates

different carnivores. The fifteen species of eared seals, sea lions, and walruses are related to a bearlike creature that lived on the coast of the North Pacific and took to the sea some twenty-four million years ago during the Oligocene Epoch. During the same period in the North Atlantic, an otterlike animal also returned to the sea to become the ancestor of the nineteen species of true seals. The two creatures evolved over millions of years to "converge" in a remarkably similar structure, ideally adapted to the amphibious nature of their lives.

The seals' evolutionary relationship to land mammals is readily seen in the skeleton. An x-ray of a seal reveals leg bones, but

Now found only off the coasts of Western and Southern Australia, in the 1700s Australian sea lions were found on islands off Northern Tasmania as well. In 1844, the Governor of South Australia reported seeing sea lions ''as large as donkeys,'' presumably males, since females like this one (left) are considerably smaller.

Northern fur seal bulls (below center) are reported to make four different sounds: a fighting challenge, said to resemble the puffing of a steam engine, a deep, hoarse roar, a growl of sorts, and the last something between a hiss and a whistle. The cows bleat.

New Zealand fur seals like this one (far left) were first identified from a ''sea bear'' sketched by the assistant naturalist on Captain Cook's 1773 voyage in search of a southern continent.

© Dominique Braud/Tom Stack & Associates

I swam with half-a-dozen sea lions at Devil's Crown, near Floreana Island in the Galapagos, including several females like this sleepy pair (right). They regarded me with exactly the same curiosity and fascination with which I regarded them, though mine was mixed with envy at the grace and speed with which they swam.

Very little is known about Galapagos fur seal's feeding and breeding habits (far right). They are believed to be closely related to the South American fur seal.

they are encased in the torpedo-shaped body up to the ankle. Eared seals can turn their hind flippers forward to walk on land; true seals hold their hind flippers up in the air and lurch, hump, wriggle, and squirm to make terrestrial progress. Walruses can turn their hind flippers forward and walk on the soles, supporting part of the upper body weight on the palms of the foreflippers like sea lions, but the walrus is so heavy that most of its weight is supported by the stomach. Basically, walruses lunge along at a moderate speed at best. On ice, crabeater seals can attain speeds of 16 miles (26 km) per hour; ribbon seals can move faster than a man can sprint; and there are several reports from polar explorers that leopard seals—unique among seals in their willingness to attack people—can move across ice at an unnerving rate.

Seals maintain a constant body temperature of 98° F. (38.5°C.) A seal pup born in the Arctic or Antarctic may leave the 98° F. (38.5° C.) warmth of its mother's body only to be expelled into a temperature of –31° F. (–35° C.), a drop of 129° F. (54°C.), which has to come as a bit of a rude welcome to the world.

Seals maintain body warmth by building up a thick layer of blubber that protects the body's core temperature exactly as the insulating layer of a thermos maintains its contents at a steady temperature. The insulating properties of blubber are estimated to be as effective as asbestos. Fur seals also gain some insulation from their thick underfur, which functions like a diver's dry suit by trapping a layer of warm air next to the skin, keeping the skin both warm and dry. Walruses, sea lions, and elephant seals huddle together, bodies piled every which way, which also conserves heat in cold weather. When push comes to shove, cold-water seals can escape the chill of ice, snow, freezing air, and cold winds by retreating to the water. Water temperature is far less variable than air temperature, rarely varying more than 9° F. (–13° C.).

For migratory and warm-water seals, escaping to the water also helps when temperatures become uncomfortably warm. Seals have few sweat glands, so sweating probably doesn't cool them off significantly. Also, because seals do not drink water, scientists speculate that what little water is derived from their food may be too precious to waste on merely cooling off.

Seals are inveterate sunbathers, given the slightest opportunity. When the weather gets excessively warm, as seals judge these things, they do as little as they can possibly arrange, becoming virtually inert. They find a shady place, fan themselves with their flippers, lie in damp sand, slide into the surf, or take a nap. Northern elephant seals flip wet sand over themselves and anyone else in the immediate vicinity. Seals native to tropical areas, such as the coast of Mexico, the Hawaiian Islands, and the Galapagos Islands, simply take a quick dip when the sun's too hot, then stretch themselves out to bask in the sun until it's time for the next quick dip. After some unavoidably strenuous exertion such as fighting or mating, sea lions have been known to plunk themselves into a nice, cool tidepool. Sunglasses and cold beer are not reported in the literature.

Chapter Two

True Seals

T he true seals are members of the family *Phocidae,* which is divided
into two tribes, the *Phocinae* and the *Monachinae*. The word *phoca*
comes from the Greek word *phoce,* meaning seal, which is itself derived from the Sanskrit root, *spha,* a word that means to swell up—referring, of
course, to the fact that most seals look as though somebody had inflated them
with a bicycle pump. *Monachinae* comes from the Greek *monachos,* meaning
monk, which derives from the rolls of fat around the seal's neck that look remarkably like a friar's cowl. They are commonly referred to as phocids and
monk seals.

Most northern phocids (*Phocinae*) are found north of the equator, many of
them in the Arctic. Southern phocids (*Monachinae*) are found south of the
equator, most of them in the Antarctic. The exceptions are the Northern elephant seal, which wanders along the west coast of North America between

T he Weddell seal (op-
posite page) can stay
under water for a full hour.
That's much longer than has
been observed in any other
seal. They were once believed
to be the deepest divers as
well, having carried a time/
depth recorder down almost
2,000 feet (600 m), but they
were recently surpassed by a
Northern elephant seal cow
that dived 4,125 feet
(1,250 m).

All seal pups must learn to swim; they are not born knowing how. Harbor seal pups like this little one can swim and dive shortly after birth, though in many species, the pups cannot swim until they are several months old.

northern California and Baja California, and the three monk seals, found in the Mediterranean, the Caribbean, and around Hawaii, which, as members of the *Monachinae* tribe, are lumped with southern phocids.

There are eighteen distinguishing characteristics between true seals (*Phocidae*) and eared seals (*Otariidae*)—primarily that true seals have no visible ears. Some scientists would feel obliged to phrase that as ''no external ear pinna'' and would likely continue on to report that other tribal characteristics include the fact that the petrobasilar vacuity is continuous with the posterior lacerate foramen and extends anteriorly, usually beyond the posterior carotid foramen. For most of us it is enough to know that there

are distinct and recognizable differences between the two.

Other identifying characteristics of true seals and eared seals include the fact that true seals are found not only in the ocean, as eared seals and sea lions are, but in estuaries and fresh water as well; their hind flippers cannot be rotated forward, so they cannot walk on land as eared seals do; both sets of flippers are furry on both sides, unlike eared seals, which have no hair on their flippers; the nails of the hind flippers are all the same size (on eared seals three are longer); the skin is dark under the fur rather than light; and females may have either two or four nipples, as opposed to eared seals, which always have four.

NORTHERN PHOCIDS

Harbor Seal

Harbor seals (*Phoca vitulina*) are found along the coasts of both the North Atlantic and the North Pacific. There are four recognized subspecies—the western Atlantic harbor seal (*Phoca vitulina concolor*), the eastern Atlantic harbor seal (*P. vitulina vitulina*), the insular seal (*P. vitulina stejnegeri*), and the Pacific harbor seal (*P. vitulina richardsi*). The harbor seal is also known as the common or spotted seal. The nostrils are set in a wide V, and in the water the harbor seal resembles nothing so much as a friendly, curious dog. A creature of coasts and shores, found in estuaries and bays, rivers and lakes, on sandbanks and rocky outcroppings, harbor seals are shore-living animals with a liking for fresh water and a dislike for ice, preferring places where rivers flowing into the sea keep it free of arctic ice.

The total world population for all species of harbor seal was 360,000 in 1983, and it is probably less today. Harbor seals are protected in the United States, the Netherlands and in some places in Norway, but they continue to be hunted in Britain, Canada, Denmark, and Sweden.

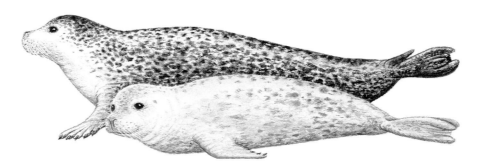

ly seen along the coasts of Newfoundland, Nova Scotia, the Gulf of St. Lawrence, and on Prince Edward Island, Sable Island, and the Magdalen Islands. It was first identified in 1842. One hundred years later, in 1942, a new subspecies, *P. vitulina mellonae,* was identified living in the landlocked fresh water Seal Lakes of the Ungava Peninsula of Labrador.

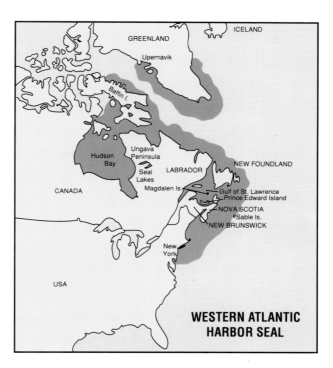

WESTERN ATLANTIC HARBOR SEAL

Note:. The gray area in each map indicates the seal's range.

Western Atlantic Harbor Seal
(P. vitulina concolor)

The western Atlantic harbor seal ranges from New York in the south to Upernavik, Greenland, and the western shores of Baffin Island in the north. It is most common from Labrador to New Brunswick and is frequent-

The fur can be almost any shade of brownish gray freckled with small black spots; it has a pale belly. The seals feed only once a day. Unlike some other seals, they do not fast while pupping, breeding, and molting.

Western Atlantic harbor seals mate in mid-June, most probably in the water. The fertilized egg divides a few times and then stops, becoming a blastocyst. The blastocyst remains in suspended animation for three months, after which it attaches to the wall of the womb. The delayed implantation allows the seals to pup and mate at the same time each year despite a nine-month gesta-

© Frank S. Balthis/Nature's Design

tion period. It also allows the females to regain their strength and weight between pregnancies. The pups, which are dark brown, are nursed for three or four weeks, after which the mother leaves and the pups gather in small groups to begin fending for themselves. These harbor seals molt in July, after the breeding season.

Western Atlantic harbor seals have few enemies, or more accurately two enemies, sharks and people. The impact of shark predation on harbor seals is negligible; the impact of hunting may reduce them to extinction. From 1927 until 1976, Canada offered a bounty on harbor seals. The United States extended full protection to harbor seals in 1972. In 1981, the International Convention on Trade and Endangered Species recommended protecting harbor seals under Appendix II of the Convention, which is designed "to avoid utilization incompatible with the survival of a species," but Canada did not support the resolution.

Eastern Atlantic Harbor Seal
(Phoca vitulina vitulina)

The eastern Atlantic harbor seal was identified by Linnaeus himself in 1758. It ranges from Britain in the south to Finland and Iceland in the north. The largest group is found on the east coast of England in the Wash, bordered by the counties of Norfolk and Lincolnshire, where there is a breeding colony of approximately 6,000 seals. Judith King reports in *Seals of the World* that all the breeding colonies in Britain combined produce about 1,900 pups annually—and 100 more than that, or 2,000 pups, are killed each year for their fur, a truly astonishing management of the resource. Adult eastern Atlantic harbor seals, which are gray-brown with black spots, are protected in Britain from June 1 to August 31, except those

The mouth of the Russian River on the Northern California coast (far left) is typical harbor seal habitat; Harbor seals like fresh water and often swim up rivers. They bask, sleep, molt, and pup on rocky islets, sand bars, flat beaches, and mud flats. The pups are born wtih the same coat as the adults, not with the baby coat that is common to most other seals.

Harbor seals are the cute, curious seals with the dog-like faces that are often seen swimming in harbors and bays. I see them from the Larkspur ferry curled up on the buoys in San Francisco Bay. They do not migrate. They choose a "home" and pretty much stay there all year round.

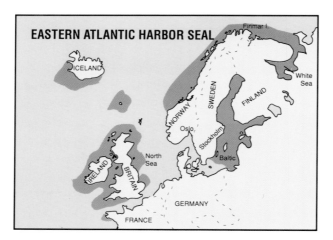

EASTERN ATLANTIC HARBOR SEAL

found in the vicinity of fishing nets and those killed for scientific or management purposes.

The pups are born on land that is exposed during low tides and are nursed both on land and in the water. Eastern Atlantic harbor seals are conscientious mothers, herding their pups into the water if threatened and even diving with them, holding them close to their chests.

The adult seals molt from mid-August to mid-September. Their bright new coats are celebrated at once with the breeding season.

These harbor seals are typically silent, but during the mating season they yelp and growl, splashing around in pairs and leaping clear out of the water. They do not form harems, nor do they appear to mate according to a dominance hierarchy.

Harbor seals along the English coast have been observed to eat some twenty-nine different kinds of fish, including flounder, sole, herring, eel, goby, cod, and whiting. They also eat shellfish—crabs, mussels, and whelks—as well as squid. Weaned pups start out with shrimp until they learn to catch fish. Harbor seals are preyed upon by polar bears, killer whales, sharks, eagles (which sometimes take the pups), and people.

An outbreak of phocine distemper virus, a disease similar to canine distemper, has devastated 75 percent of the eastern Atlantic harbor seal population along the coasts of Great Britain, West Germany, Holland, and Denmark. Major rescue and treatment efforts have been mounted in the North Sea in England and at a nursery for seals in Pieterburen in Holland.

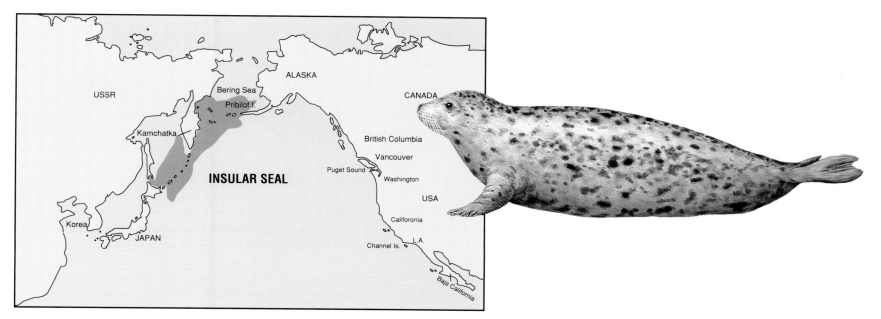

Insular Seal
(*Phoca vitulina stejnegeri*)

Found in Japan on the Nemuro Peninsula in the south, the insular seal ranges north to the Soviet Union's Kuril Islands, the east coast of Kamchatka, and the Commander Islands.

The insular seal is the largest of the North Pacific harbor seals. Either pale or dark brown, they always have black spots and are very blond around the face and eyes. Insular seals breed gathered in groups of several hundred. The pups are born on rocky islets.

Pacific Harbor Seal
(*Phoca vitulina richardsi*)

The Pacific harbor seal lives along the Pacific coast and on coastal islands from Baja California at Cedros Island to the Pribilof Islands in the Bering Sea near Alaska. It is a dark, spotted seal with a light face.

Pacific harbor seals congregate on sand bars, mud flats, and rocks at low tide during the breeding season. Dark, spotted pups are born in early February in Baja California, in March and April in the Channel Islands off the California coast at Santa Barbara, in May along the coast of Washington, and from the end of June to September around Puget Sound and British Columbia. Farther north, in the Gulf of Alaska, the pups are born between May and June, and in the Pribilof Islands between June and July. They weigh around 22 pounds (10 kg) at birth. At weaning, some six weeks later, the pups will have more than doubled their weight to around 53 pounds (24 kg).

Oceanic Society Expeditions in San Francisco, California runs tours to Southeast Alaska, Vancouver Island in British Columbia , the Farallon Islands off San Francisco, and San Martin Island off Baja California, Mexico to see harbor seals (as well as other seals, whales, dolphins, and sea birds). Call (415) 441-1106 for more information and booking.

Females mate after weaning, and the blastocyst remains in suspended animation for two months before attaching to the uterine wall. Females begin breeding at three years of age, males at five.

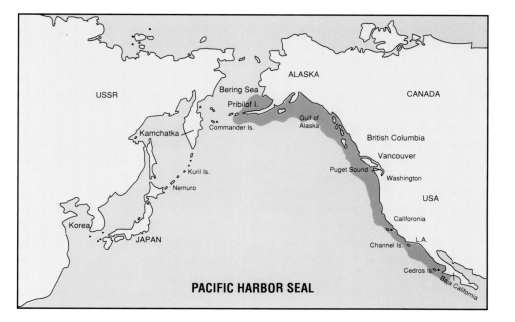

Pacific harbor seals eat squid, fish, and eels. Despite the fact that they are protected, many are shot by fishermen because they take salmon. Salmon are heavily fished along the Pacific coast, and as catches decline, seals have been presented as a likely scapegoat. In fact, studies conducted at the mouth of the Rogue River in Oregon showed that the seals' diet consists of 87 percent lamprey eels, 11 percent unidentified species, and 2 percent salmon. Since lamprey are parasites of salmon, biologists believe that by taking lamprey in such great quantity, the seals *benefit* the salmon, allowing their numbers to increase rather than decline. Studies conducted in British Columbia indicate that the amount of salmon eaten by both harbor seals and sea lions amounts to only 2.5 percent of the annual commercial catch.

Harbor seals often plunk themselves where the tide can wash over them, like children sitting and playing in the waves.

Larga Seal

(Phoca largha)

The larga has recently been promoted from a subspecies of the harbor seal to full species status. Unlike the harbor seals, the largas breed on pack ice, and the pups are born with the woolly white baby fur that harbor seal pups shed before birth.

The southernmost point of the larga's range may be as far south as the Yangtze River in China; it is certainly found in the

Yellow Sea off Korea. To the north it is found from Point Barrow to the Pribilof Islands and Aleutian Islands of Alaska. It is seen in the Sea of Japan, the Sea of Okhotsk, the Bering Sea, and the Chukchi Sea, as well as the Yellow Sea.

Largas are slightly smaller than the Pacific harbor seals. The fur is pale gray, almost silver, shading to a darker gray along the back and covered with black oval spots. Young largas are lighter colored around the eyes and nose than adults. Largas pair off to breed, each couple choosing a place well separated from other breeding pairs. Pups are born on ice floes and nurse for three weeks, tripling their birth weight in the process. The pups weigh about 20 pounds (9 kg) at birth and 62 pounds (28 kg) a month later. Their fur is white, for camouflage on the ice, and woolly.

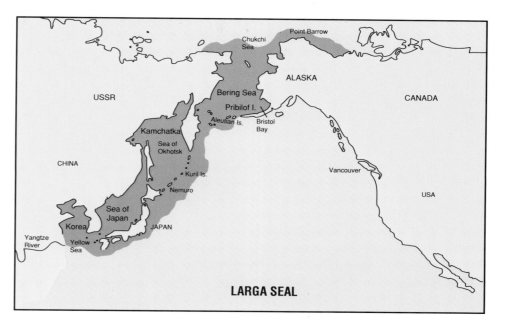

LARGA SEAL

© C. Allan Morgan

Like Pacific harbor seals the largas' whelping season is determined by latitude, with pups born earliest in the more southerly parts of the range, latest in the far northern reaches. The first pups are born from early February to mid-March. In the southern Sea of Okhotsk and Tatar Strait, pups are born in March; in the Bering Sea between late March and early May; in the northern Sea of Okhotsk, in mid-April.

Ringed Seal

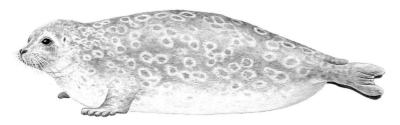

(Phoca hispida)

The most common seal of the Arctic, ringed seals are circumpolar. They are found in open water on fast ice, even as far north as the North Pole. They may be seen on the arctic coasts of Alaska, Canada, the Soviet Union, and Europe, as well as Iceland, Spitsbergen, Newfoundland, and Baffin Island. Though they are found from Japan to northern Europe, ringed seals do not migrate. In Finland and the Soviet Union they are found in the freshwater lakes, Lake Saimaa and Lake Ladoga, but there is no evidence that they ever leave the lakes to go to sea.

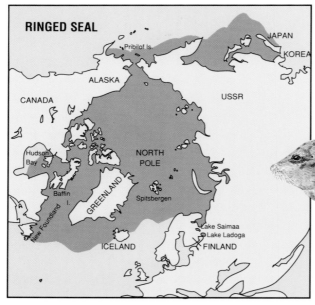

Ringed seals are light gray spotted with black, and their belly is silver. Their pups are born in oval lairs dug out of the snow on the ice. The lairs have breathing holes, so the seals can enter from the water and es-

cape into the water as well. The seals scrape out the breathing holes with the claws of their foreflippers, sometimes digging through ice more than 6 feet (2 m) thick. Polar bears and arctic foxes are both known to dig out the lairs and eat the young seals. On the ice, the pups may also be attacked by rogue walruses, and in the water killer whales are a threat to ringed seals. When it is one month old, the pup sheds its white baby skin for a beautiful coat that is dark gray on the back and silver on the belly. The pups are then called "silver jars" and are hunted for their lovely fur.

Ringed seal males declare themselves ready to mate by giving off a perfectly vile smell from March until May. The smell is so bad that "foetida" (Latin for "stinking") was once used to identify the species, which seems a bit unfair to the females. Breeding occurs in mid-April, not long after the pups are born. The blastocyst is not implanted for nearly three months, in early July. Gestation lasts nine months. Males begin breeding at seven years, females at five.

Ringed seals eat plankton, primarily, as well as small shrimps and fish.

It is impossible to estimate the total population of ringed seals, simply because they are found in so many places. Educated guesses place the figure at several million, though they are hunted intensively and many thousands are killed each year. They nearly disappeared at Lake Saimaa, in Finland, where the population fell to forty, but they are now protected there and had increased to two hundred or so by 1966, when they were last counted.

Caspian Seal

(Phoca caspica)

Found only in the Caspian Sea, the Caspian seal is descended from seals that swam in the Parathyan Sea twenty million years ago. Five to six million years ago mountains thrust up that cut the Parathys off from the Tethys, an equatorial sea that linked the Atlantic and Indian oceans. Those mountains separated the Caspian, Black, and Aral seas into enormous salt lakes.

Caspian seals are dark gray on top and dirty white underneath. They are pretty well spotted on the back, with males having more spots than females.

The annual migration of the Caspian seal extends the length of the sea from the south to the ice floes of the northeastern corner in November and December. Heavy winds tilt the floes up against each other, making a safe place for the seals to bear their young.

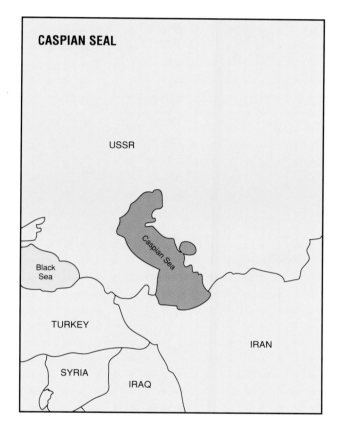

CASPIAN SEAL

The mother seals begin to molt even while they are still nursing their pups. Adult males molt at the end of March, and the young seals a little earlier. Caspian seals pair up to mate at the beginning of March, so scientists speculate that they may be monogamous. Females can breed at the age of five, but most do not until they are six or seven. Males reach sexual maturity at six or seven.

Caspian seals eat small crustaceans, sprats, herring, sand smelts, roach, carp, gobies, and even, somehow, the spiny sculpin. Sculpins are, in fact, their favorite food, which is a lot like eating needles for breakfast. Still, scientists report that, given the opportunity, Caspian seals will gorge themselves to death on sculpin.

Caspian seals are somewhat protected; it is illegal to take pregnant females and immature seals. Between 60,000 and 65,000 pups are killed annually.

Baikal Seal

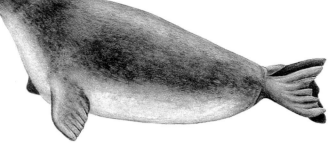

(Phoca sibirica)

The Baikal seal is found only in the Soviet Union, in Lake Baikal, the deepest lake in the world, with an average depth of 2,275 feet (700 m). At its deepest, it is a little over one mile deep (1.7 km). The seals are most often seen around the northeastern end of the lake in June when they haul themselves out on the shore. When the ice forms in October, they retreat to the water for the winter, since the water is warmer than the air. They breathe through holes in the ice until February.

Pregnant females spend the winter on the ice in lairs they build under the snow. The pups have a long white woolly coat, which they lose after two weeks, molting into a pale version of the adult dark brownish-gray coat.

Mating and molting both take place in May and June, which sounds a little like going to the prom with your hair in curlers. Females begin breeding at six years of age, males at eight, and polygamy is believed to be the order of the day.

Baikal seals are small, only a little over four feet (1.3 m) long at maturity, which is about the size of a newborn walrus or elephant seal. They eat fish and, as a result, have incurred the wrath of local fishermen.

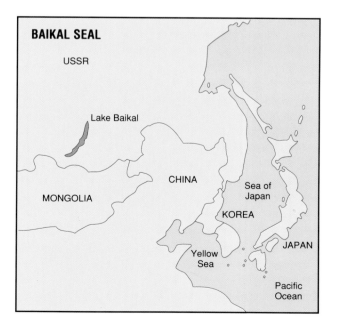

BAIKAL SEAL

The total population is estimated at between 40,000 and 50,000 seals, a tremendous recovery since the 1930s, when they were hunted almost to extinction. Some 2,000 to 3,000 pups are killed every year for their skins.

Harp seals

(Phoca groenlandica)

Harp seals are probably the most famous seals in the world: photos of baby harp seals, pudgy little white faces with huge dark eyes that are irresistably appealing, have graced the posters of wildlife conservation organizations all over the world. Until very recently, the whitecoats, as baby harp seals are called, were hunted mercilessly for their thick, soft fur. International outcry at this slaughter of the innocents—and the EEC ban on imported sealskin which eliminated the major market for whitecoat pelts—brought the hunt to a halt in 1988. Today visitors from all over the world come every March to the harp seal nurseries on the pack ice off the Magdalen Islands in the Gulf of St. Lawrence to observe and play with the baby seals.

Probably the most famous seals in the world, harp seal pups did for wildlife preservation around the world what Smoky the Bear did for American forests. People rallied to the cause of saving the harp seals by refusing to buy sealskin products. It was—and is—a joyous demonstration that people *can* live in peaceful coexistence with other species on this planet.

Creatures of the sea and ice, harp seals spend their entire lives, an average of 30 years, without ever touching land. The pups are born in February and March, nurse for twelve days, and are then abandoned by their mothers to learn to swim and forage by themselves. Harp seals migrate 3,000 miles (4827 km) each year, one of the longest migrations known for any animal. The pups migrate 1,500 miles (2414 km) north to the summer feeding grounds alone by making their way from ice pan to ice pan. Except for that first perilous and solitary year, harp seals feed, migrate, pup, and molt in large groups called pods. The name harp seal derives from the black wishbone-shaped markings on the adults that some poetic seafaring soul thought looked like an Irish harp.

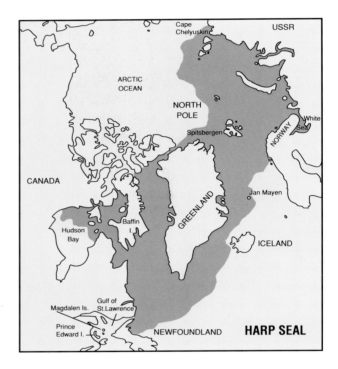

A nineteenth-century sealer recounted seeing harp seals in such numbers that they "filled the sea from the landwash seaward to the limit of his vision, and took ten days and ten nights to pass." Earlier in this century, the Canadian writer and wildlife photographer, Fred Bruemmer, reported having once rowed across a fjord in Labrador and "beneath [the boat] . . . in serried ranks swam capelin, a steady stream of life nine miles across." Today the harp seals are much reduced due to hunting; the capelin, one of the fish upon which they feed, much reduced by commercial fishing. Fishermen are inclined to blame the seals for the reduced numbers of fish, but historical accounts make it clear that before the massive sea hunts of this century and the last there were many millions more harp seals *and* many millions more fish. Researchers on both the Atlantic and Pacific coasts of North America have begun to speculate that in the natural order of things, seals contributed to *increased* numbers of fish, a point of view the commercial fishing industry has been slow to see despite the substantial historical and contemporary evidence.

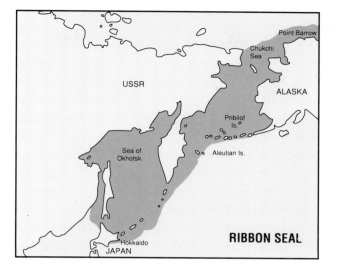

RIBBON SEAL

Ribbon seals are sleeker than most arctic seals, with a long, slim, flexible neck. When disturbed, they stretch their necks as regally as swans and hold their heads high to look around, but since their eyesight in air is not good, they are easy to approach. They are elegantly sinuous and extremely fast on ice, able to go as fast as a man can sprint.

Almost nothing is known of what they eat, though it is believed that they eat arctic cod, pollock, and eelpout as well as shrimp and crab.

Physiologically, the ribbon seal presents another mystery. The males possess a curious air sac between their throats and their lungs about 1½ feet (43 cm) long. It is unique to the ribbon seal—no other seal has anything even remotely resembling such a thing—and no one knows what it is for. It has been suggested that, inflated, the sac could create greater buoyancy for a species that lives so much of its life at sea, but that does not explain why only males have it.

Pups are born on the ice in April and early May; they weigh about 23 pounds (10.5 kg) and are not quite three feet (90 cm) long. They nurse for almost a month, by which time they have doubled in weight. Like harp seals, the pups are left unattended during this period, though their mothers are usually in the water close by; also like harp seals, they are weaned abruptly when the mother leaves. Mother ribbon seals do feed during the nursing period, unlike harp seals, though the pups must learn to dive and feed by themselves. Molting takes place any time between the end of March and the end of July.

While no one knows for sure, these mysterious and beautiful creatures are believed to live between twenty and thirty years. The Soviet Union hunts ribbon seals and took 13,000 annually in the seven years between 1961 and 1967. This reduced the population

Ribbon Seal

(Phoca fasciata)

Ribbon seals are far and away the most striking of all seals. The pandas of the sea, they are a dark chocolate brown with broad white ribbons aound the neck, each foreflipper, and the hindquarters. They are mysterious creatures, found on the pack ice of the Okhotsk, the Bering, and the Chukchi seas. When the ice melts, these beautiful, solitary creatures disappear, no one knows where. Educated guesses suggest they live at sea, for they are only rarely seen on land. From north to south, their range extends from Point Barrow in Alaska to the Aleutians and Hokkaido's northern coast, in Japan.

dangerously, and a new quota of 3,000 seals annually was established, which has allowed the population to recover somewhat. There are approximately 240,000 ribbon seals in the world, 140,000 in the Sea of Okhotsk and 100,000 in the Bering Sea.

HOODED SEAL

Hooded Seal

(Cystophora cristata)

If ribbon seals are the most beautiful of seals, hooded seals are surely the most bizarre. The males have a hood, a fold of skin that extends from just behind the eyes and dangles, when slack, in front of the mouth. Inflated, it looks like a large, dark brown plastic cushion, approximately twice the size of a football, smack on top of the seal's

A s attractive as these hooded seal bulls (above) undoubtedly are to the cows of their kind, they are not truly serious about courtship until they blow a large red balloon out their left nostril. Think of it as the hooded seal equivalent of presenting her with an engagement ring. Believe it or not, they have beautiful babies.

head. As if that were not peculiar enough, the male also blows a bright red balloon out its left nostril, about the size of an ostrich egg. Both the hood and the balloon are inflated in courtship. What girl could resist?

Hooded seals are gray with black splotches and patches. They are found in the North Atlantic and Arctic seas, on drifting ice floes and in deep water, shunning both land and pack ice. Essentially solitary, they gather in February to pup and breed and again in the summer (June, July, and possibly August) to molt. Beyond these gatherings little is known of how hooded seals live. They share their range with the harp seal, and whelping and breeding patches as well. There are three main herds, one on the Front, off the east coast of Canada; one on the West Ice, off the island of Jan Mayen east of Greenland; and one in the Davis Strait between Greenland and Canada.

All hooded seals give birth at the same time each year, during the last two weeks of March. The mother seal selects an isolated place on an ice floe at least 150 feet (50 m) from any other seal. Unlike harp seals, which pop out pups like peas from a pod, hooded seals have a long labor, and at 44 pounds (20 kg) the pups are more than twice the size at birth of harp seal pups. They are also much more advanced in physical development, with a thin blubber layer, and able to crawl and swim soon after birth.

The hooded seal's milk is one of the richest of all marine mammals, more than 50 percent fat. The pups nurse for only four days, the shortest lactation period known for any mammal, and still they more than double their birth weight, gaining an astonishing 11 pounds (5 kg) a day.

Hooded seals select their mates after whelping, so the female is joined by a male during the nursing period. These trios—male, female, and pup—are often referred to as families, but as researchers Kit Kovacs and David Lavigne point out, "This is a misnomer because the male is almost certainly not the father of this year's pup, although he undoubtedly aspires to be the father of next year's pup."

Mother hoods never leave their pups during the four days of nursing and defend them fiercely. Many a sealer's log records their fearless devotion to their youngsters. The females also defend their pups from courting males who, in the heat of their rivalry, sometimes fail to watch out for a pup. Despite the difference in size and the ferocity of the rival males, the females have no trouble driving off males that get dangerously close to the little ones, and do not hesitate to do so.

The pups are extraordinarily beautiful, with a luxuriantly thick coat that is blue-gray on the top and silver-gray underneath. Its beauty once made this the most valuable fur in the sealing industry and gave the baby hoods their nickname of "blueback."

Hooded seals live thirty-five years, assuming they escape their natural enemies: polar bears, Greenland sharks, killer whales, and the greatest predator of all, humans. Some 15,000 seals are killed annually by hunters from Canada and Norway.

Grey Seal

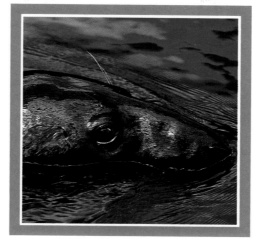

(Halichoerus grypus)

Grey seals have an enormous range, extending from the Gulf of St. Lawrence in Canada to Iceland, Great Britain, and the Baltic. They are found in both temperate and subarctic seas. Hunted so mercilessly for oil in the nineteenth century that they were believed extinct in Canadian waters, they have been hunted equally mercilessly in the twentieth century as a carrier of codworm. Despite the fact that codworm poses no danger to humans who consume codfish, and despite the fact that grey seals were recommended for the endangered species list in 1981, several countries, including Canada, Scotland, Sweden, and Finland, still fund government-sponsored kills and pay substantial bounties with their citizens' taxes. Grey seals are fully protected in the United States under special legislation passed in 1965 and under the Marine Mammal Act of

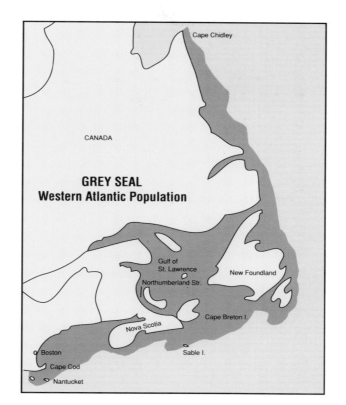

GREY SEAL
Western Atlantic Population

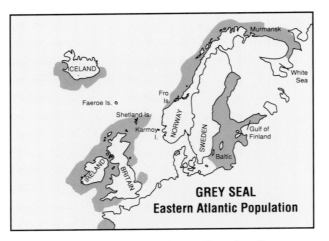

GREY SEAL
Eastern Atlantic Population

The grey seal was believed extinct in North America by many wildlife biologists until a colony was found in New Brunswick, Canada at the mouth of the Miramichi River in 1949. They were a choice display for zoos like the Cincinnatti Zoo where this sleepy one was photographed.

1972 and in Great Britain under the Conservation of Seals Act of 1970, though this act still permits killing seals and commercial hunting of the "population surplus," whatever that means in a species that's been recommended for the endangered species list.

Grey seals bear their pups on islands and on fast ice in the cold months of the year, which may vary from September to March, depending on where the breeding grounds are located. The birth is very rapid, and the pups, covered with long silky white hair, weigh about 31 pounds (14 kg). They shed this lovely coat after three weeks. Despite their name, grey seals may be a wide variety of colors from brown to gray to silver, and all the shades in between. Whatever basic color they are, males are dark with light spots and females are light with dark spots. Pups show this color difference as soon as they shed their baby fur.

Grey seal mothers nurse only their own pups, which they identify by voice and smell. The pups feed for six minutes every five or six hours and gain 3⅓ pounds (1.5 kg) a day. They nurse for three weeks. By the time they are finished, they weigh 110 pounds (50 kg) and look as fat as a baby blimp, especially since they are no longer than the 30 inches (76 cm) they were at birth.

Grey seal pups can swim from the time they are born, but most of them don't until they have completed the molt that occurs when they are a month old. Pups may go to sea immediately after weaning or spend a month or more on land before venturing off across a wide range. One tagged on the

Farne Islands at a week of age was recovered on the Frø Islands 595 miles (960 km) away when it was nine weeks old. Another tagged on the Farne Islands when it was a month old was found at Karmøy, Norway, nine days later; it had gone 360 miles (580 km), swimming an average of 40 miles (64 km) a day. A three-week-old pup tagged at Sable Island in eastern Canada turned up at Barnegat Light, New Jersey, some 795 miles (1,280 km) away 25 days later.

Grey seal bulls select their territories on breeding beaches about a month before the first pups are born. The biggest bulls get the best territories—which gives them first shot at the females. Younger, smaller bulls get the fringes. The females are ready to mate when the pup is no longer nursing, and mating takes place both on land and in the water. The seals return each year to the breeding grounds of their birth.

Grey seals fast during pupping and breeding, and the females may lose as much as 25 percent of their body weight in a month. Twenty-nine species of fish have been identified as part of their diet, as have crabs and shrimp. The seals eat bottom-feeding fish from depths of at least 230 feet (70 m). They can dive as deep as 700 feet (213 m) and stay down as long as twenty-three minutes. Where salmon are fished commercially, grey seals are not popular among fishermen, who do not much care for efficient and effective competitors.

Bearded Seal

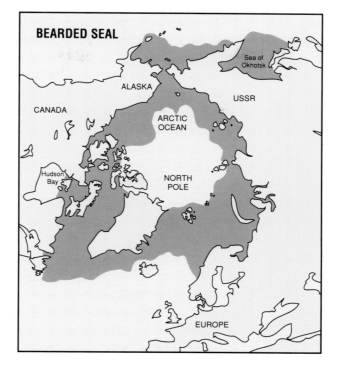

(Erignathus barbatus)

Bearded seals haven't got beards exactly; they have long, glistening white mustaches that curl in spirals at the tip. They are the largest of the arctic seals (except, of course, the walrus), more than 7 feet (2.25 m) long and weighing in at 550 pounds (250 kg). They are circumpolar and can be found along the coasts of all the continents that border the Arctic Ocean: Europe, Asia, and North America.

Bearded seals have the dreadful dilemma of being both very curious and very wary. Whenever they are on land or ice, they stay close enough to the water to make a fast escape. That may be because their response to being frightened is to become paralyzed with fear, so they cannot risk having far to go to get away. Their only real enemies are polar bears and people. The seals are an important source of food for arctic natives and are hunted commercially by the Soviets.

Bearded seals are seldom seen in large groups, even during the breeding season. Pups are born on ice floes and are closely guarded by mothers, who stay close to the pups and defend them vigorously from harm. Mating takes place after the pups are weaned. After mating comes the molt.

Both males and females have identical coats, an unremarkable dark gray on the back and an equally unremarkable light gray on the stomach. During courtship, the males sing a long warbling note that ends in a soft moan or a sigh, an appropriate sort of sound for a love song.

Bearded seals eat bottom fish, such as flounder, sculpin, and polar cod, crab and shrimp, and other shellfish such as clams and whelks. Whelks, in fact, are a special favorite, and since no whelk shells are ever found in their stomachs, it is assumed that they suck the whelks out of their shells very much as walrus do.

Because they never gather in significant numbers and range so widely, there are no reliable population estimates. Scientists place the number at 500,000 worldwide.

SOUTHERN PHOCIDS

Mediterranean Monk Seal

(Monachus monachus)

Considering that the Mediterranean monk seal has been known for 3,000 years, it's astonishing how little specific information there is about it. Homer, Pliny, and Plutarch wrote about it; Aristotle dissected one and left a remarkably accurate account of its

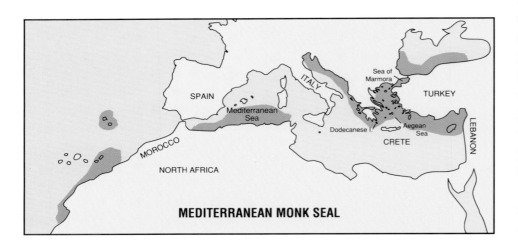

MEDITERRANEAN MONK SEAL

anatomy. Coins dating from 500 B.C. carry its likeness. They were once abundant throughout the Mediterranean and Aegean seas on the islands and coasts of Italy, Greece, Turkey, Bulgaria, Yugoslavia, Morocco, Algeria, Tunisia, Lebanon, Cyprus, and even Spanish Sahara, and were found on the coasts of France, Spain, the Crimea, Israel, and Egypt—but no longer. Today the greatest concentration of Mediterranean monk seals is found in the Greek islands, and that herd is estimated at perhaps two hundred; the total worldwide population is somewhere between five hundred and one thousand seals and is almost certainly declining.

The Mediterranean monk seal is extremely susceptible to water pollution, and its native waters have become more and more heavily polluted as the century has progressed. Its natural habitat is sandy beaches, and as these beaches are also preferred by people, the seal has been supplanted by sunbathers. Notice of its dire plight has captured international awareness in the last few years. Greece is planning a series of reserves in the Dodecanese Islands, and Turkey has proposed a reserve on the Kapidaz Peninsula in the Sea of Marmara.

Almost nothing is known about its life history; as an animal on the verge of extinction, it is a doctoral dissertation waiting to happen, a scien-

tific reputation waiting to be made. No one knows how long Mediterranean monk seals live, where they migrate (if they migrate), how they conduct their courtship rituals, whether they are monogamous or polygamous, when they mate, where they mate, how long they are pregnant, how they care for their pups, what sounds they make, what, precisely, they eat, how much they eat, when or where they molt (if they molt), et cetera.

What *is* known is that the pups are born in caves or grottoes, most of them during September or October, though newborns have been found from May to November. They have black woolly baby fur, which they molt at six weeks of age. The molt is believed to coincide with weaning, but no one knows for certain. Adult seals are nearly black on the back, lighter on the underside, sometimes with a large white patch on the belly.

The Mediterranean monk seal eats fish and octopus. Scientists speculate that it may not be able to dive very deeply since fishermen seldom complain of seal raids on nets set deeper than 100 feet (30 m).

West Indian Monk Seal
(*Monachus tropicalis*)

The West Indian monk seal is believed to be extinct, since no one has seen one since 1952. A small hope is upheld by reports of animals that might have been monk seals spotted in the East Bahamas in the 1970s, but a search in 1979 did not turn up a single one.

Little is known about them, despite the fact that they were reported as early as 1494, when Columbus recorded in the log of his second voyage that his men killed eight "sea wolves" asleep on the sand at an anchorage off Haiti. They were not even given the dignity of a scientific name until more than three and a half centuries later. West Indian monk seals were hunted to extinction for their oil.

Still, on the off chance that you might see one on your next vacation to the Caribbean, the adults are 6½ to 8 feet (2–2.4 m) long, gray-brown on the back, creamy white on the belly. Pups are black and born at the beginning of December. If you spot one, get photos if you can, note the location precisely, and report it to a good scientific institution such as the West Indies Institute at Christiansted, St. Croix, U.S. Virgin Islands.

Hawaiian Monk Seal

(*Monachus schauinslandi*)

Found only on the leeward chain of the Hawaiian Islands, Hawaiian monk seals are completely protected; in addition, all of the islands in the leeward chain are included in the Hawaiian Islands National Wildlife Refuge. But that still may not be enough to save them from extinction. The seals breed on four atolls: Pearl and Hermes Reef, Lisianski Island, Laysan Island, and French Frigates Shoal. While it is difficult to determine population figures precisely where there are so many tiny islets, from counts made at the breeding grounds, it appears that the population is declining at all of the whelping

Hawaiian monk seals (far left bottom) are seriously endangered, with only 700 believed left in the world. They are found only in the Leeward Chain of the Hawaiian Islands, which has been declared a wildlife refuge for the seals and many rare species of birds. No one other than authorized researchers are permitted on the islands of the Leeward Chain.

WEST INDIAN MONK SEAL

USA

MEXICO

Gulf of Mexico

Bahama Is.

CUBA

JAMAICA

Caribbian Sea

NICARAGUA

COSTA RICA

This Hawaiian monk seal pup could swim by the time it was four days old. Pups are born on sandy beaches well above the high tide line. They lose their baby coats of soft black fur when they are about a month old.

© Jacki Kilbride/EarthViews

patches except French Frigates Shoal. Until about twenty-five years ago, the Hawaiian monk seal also whelped on Kure and Midway islands at the northwestern tip of the leeward chain, but constant human disturbance drove them away. In the past twenty-five years the population has declined by 50 percent, and the total population is estimated at only seven hundred.

Hawaiian monk seals are dark gray on the top and light gray, almost silver, on the bottom. The pups are black, molting their baby coat when they are about a month old. Adult females are almost 8 feet (2.3 m) long, larger than the males by about a foot (30 cm). They also outweigh the males substantially, by some 220 pounds (100 kg). They weigh close to 600 pounds (273 kg), while the males weigh in at 381 pounds (173 kg).

The females fast during nursing and lose most of the weight difference then. They stay with their pups constantly. The mothers typically lose 4½ pounds (2 kg) for every 2.2 pounds (1 kg) the pup gains. Put another way, the pup gains 99 pounds (45 kg) during the six weeks it nurses, while mom loses 198 pounds (90 kg). Pups weigh 35 pounds

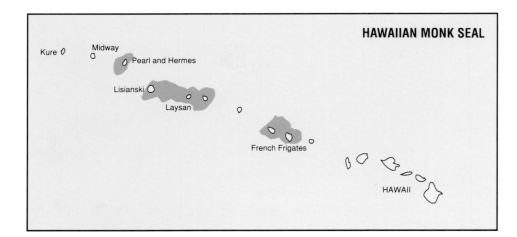

HAWAIIAN MONK SEAL

Kure
Midway
Pearl and Hermes
Lisianski
Laysan
French Frigates
HAWAII

(16 kg) at birth, double their birth weight in seventeen days, and quadruple it by the time they're weaned six weeks later.

Pups can swim from the time they are four days old. After weaning, the pup lives off its blubber layer until it learns to fend for itself.

The pups may be born any time between the end of December and August 15, but the majority are born between March 15 and May 31. They are born on coral sand beaches, well beyond the high tide line. Pregnant females gather on quiet, protected beaches to bear and nurse their pups. The mothers put up with each other, but courting males are firmly rejected. In fact, mating has never been observed; however, since the females have pups, it may be safely assumed that it does occur.

Most of the males molt in June, the females, after their pups are weaned. Like elephant seals, Hawaiian monk seals shed both skin and hair. The literature does not report whether they look and smell as bad as elephant seals do during this process.

Hawaiian monk seals feed at night, largely because the creatures they eat are nocturnal, and in shallow waters, because they feed mainly on bottom-dwellers. They eat eels, octopus, and other reef fish. Their diet may be partially responsible for the precipitous decline in the Hawaiian monk seal population over the last twenty years. In 1978 a great many seals died of ciguatoxin poisoning. Ciguatoxin is produced by a protozoan that concentrates in fish up through the marine food chain, making the fish extremely poisonous to mammals. It occurs where coral reefs have been disturbed, and researchers suspect that the blasting of reefs at Midway Island, Hawaii, may have caused the outbreak of ciguatoxin.

Sharks are Hawaiian monk seals' natural enemy, and they take significant numbers. In addition, many seals are injured or killed by becoming entangled in abandoned fishing nets.

The Hawaiian monk seal has exactly the same body temperature as arctic seals, and a thick blubber layer as well. It adapts to the warm temperatures at the opposite end of the thermometer by becoming virtually inert during the day, lying in the shade or damp sand whenever possible, and restricting serious activity, such as feeding, to the cooler hours of darkness. Mostly they do as most of us do in Hawaii: lie on the beach a lot and catch a few waves every once in a while.

Weddell Seal

(Leptonychotes wedelli)

Weddell seals are engagingly and openly curious. They are among those wild animals, too few and far between, that have no fear of people and are more likely to roll over on their side and wave a foreflipper than to try to escape. Scientists have not hesitated to take advantage of this fact. Experiments done on Weddell seals with time and depth recorders established the Weddell for many years as the world champion diver, going to depths of 1,969 feet (600 m), and staying down as long as a full hour. The record for depth now belongs to a female northern elephant seal that dived to 4,200 feet (1,292 m), but Weddells are still the undisputed champs for length of time submerged. Can you imagine what it's like to know you might not get dinner unless you held your breath for an hour?

Fish make up 50 percent of the Weddell seals' diet, some of considerable size. Researchers watched one Weddell seal drag a fish close to five feet (1.5 m) long and more than 68 pounds (31 kg) up through a breathing hole onto the antarctic ice and settle in for a satisfying three-hour feast. It repeated the performance the following evening. Weddell seals also eat shrimp and squid.

These seals are the all-time southerners; no seal—indeed few creatures of any sort—is found any farther south or closer to the South Pole. It is truly a creature of Antarctica, found mainly on the fast ice within sight of land. They do not migrate in the conventional sense of deliberately traveling from one location to another in search of a more amiable climate or richer food supply; they *do* move with the ice front, heading north in winter, south in the spring. Some seals stay in the south all winter, where temperatures may be −4° F. (−20° C.). This tem-

Weddell seals live on the shores of Antarctica, as far south as open water allows without migrating. While all Weddell seals have splashes and streaks of white on a black coat (the belly is pretty much all white), this pup is a rare albino.

perature does not, of course, include wind chill factor. (For a clearer understanding of antarctic wind and weather, read *Endurance* by Alfred Lansing, the story of Sir Ernest Shackleton's antarctic exploration, and *Mawson's Will* by Lennard Bickel, the story of Sir Douglas Mawson's expedition. One apprehends at once why Antarctica must remain forever undeveloped; it is, in the truest sense, a howling wilderness.) Water temperature is significantly warmer, 30° F. (–1° C.), though it is covered in winter by ice many feet thick. The seals spend the seven or eight months of winter in the water beneath the dark antarctic ice, coming to breathing holes for air. They keep the breathing holes open by gnawing at the ice with their teeth. They are rather buck-

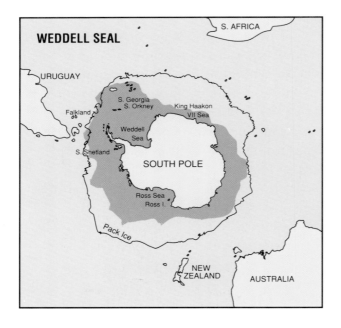

WEDDELL SEAL

S. AFRICA
URUGUAY
S. Georgia
S. Orkney
King Haakon
VII Sea
Falkland
Weddell
Sea
S. Shetland
SOUTH POLE
Ross Sea
Ross I.
Pack Ice
NEW
ZEALAND
AUSTRALIA

toothed, which makes it somewhat easier to scrape away at the ice over their heads. Ordinarily only one seal will use a breathing hole at a time. If two arrive simultaneously, one will leave among a curious chatter of trills, chirps, and a rapid clattering of teeth.

Female Weddell seals are slightly larger than the males, a difference of 8½ feet (2.6 m) versus 8¼ feet (2.5 m). One large female was measured at 10½ feet (3.2 m) and weighed in at 904 pounds (411 kg), but this record is considered to be the exception rather than the norm. They are black on the back with white streaks along the sides, gray on the bottom with white streaks, and have a small head and a heart-shaped face like a cat. In the summer, they turn a rusty gray-brown. Weddell seals molt during the Antarctic summer, between December and March. They do not fast during the molt, as many seals do.

Pups are born on the Antarctic mainland, on the southern Shetland Islands and the southern Orkney Islands, and at Larsen Harbor, South Georgia. Pregnant cows haul themselves out on the sea ice a few days before their pups are born. They give each other a wide berth and try to find a spot near a lead of open water. The pups are gray with a dark stripe down the back and lose their baby fur when they are two weeks old.

Pups are about five feet (1.5 m) long and weigh 64 pounds (29 kg) at birth. They nurse for six to seven weeks, doubling their weight in ten days. They weigh 242 pounds (110 kg) by the time they're weaned. The pups start swimming as early as eight days old, and small shrimp are part of their diet long before weaning.

The pups stick close to their mothers for the first two weeks, going to the edge of the ice with her and waiting there for several hours until she returns. No one knows if the mother seal feeds while she is gone, but there is no evidence to suggest that she does. Once the pups are a couple of weeks old, both mother and child spend some time in the water during the day, and most take to the water for the night as well. The mothers take good care of their pups, snapping aggressively and defending their little ones from intruders.

The seals mate toward the end of the nursing period. Adult bulls do battle for their lady fair and sport many a wound and scar as evidence of the depth of their passion. Mating has been observed only once, and on that occasion it took place underwater. Only after the breeding season do the breeding seals permit the rowdy adolescent males to come into the rookery.

One of the advantages to living in a place so inhospitable to life is that there are relatively few predators. Killer whales may attack Weddell seals, but even that is not known for certain.

Population figures are hard to come by for a seal that wanders so far and wide. Estimates are made by flying over and counting the seals in a relatively small area and extrapolating that figure for the entire polar ice cap and surrounding seas. It is a method that leaves a great deal to be desired in precision and accuracy, but until something better suggests itself, there is nothing else to go by. There are believed to be 50,000 Weddell seals in the western Ross Sea and a total worldwide population of between 250,000 and 500,000, though some researchers believe these figures to be conservative.

Under the Convention for the Conservation of Antarctic Seals of 1978, Weddell seals are fully protected when they are on fast ice; there is a closed season on sealing between March 1 and August 31; there are six sealing zones, one of which will be off-limits each year in rotation; and three Seal Reserves are established where no seals of any species may be captured or killed. The Convention also sets annual kill quotas, should a seal hunting industry develop in the Antarctic. The quota for Weddell seals is 5,000.

Life in the floe lane. Weddell seals are the most numerous Antarctic seal after the Crabeater seal with a population estimated at half a million.

© Gerry Ellis/Ellis Wildlife Collection

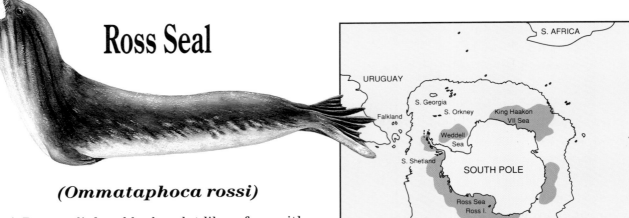

Ross Seal

ROSS SEAL

(Ommataphoca rossi)

A Ross seal's head looks a lot like a frog with the mumps, with bulging eyes and a thick neck that always appears swollen under the chin. Its huge, dark eyes gave it its scientific name: the Latin translates as Ross's big-eyed seal. In fact, it has the largest eyes of any seal, 2⅓ inches (60 mm) in diameter. Only the southern elephant seal comes close to having eyes as big.

Ross seals—named after Sir James Clark Ross, commander of the HMS *Erebus* of the British expedition to the Antarctic of 1839 through 1843—are found only in the Antarctic, most often on small, smooth floes of pack ice. Since the *Erebus* was the first ship to force her way through the pack ice of the Ross Sea, the name seems particularly apt. More often seen alone than in herds, the greatest concentrations are found in the

King Haakon VII Sea and in the Ross Sea, though they are seen throughout the Antarctic.

Silver-gray on the back and almost white on the belly, the chest is pale gray marked with darker gray parallel stripes.

The Ross seal produces a whole range of chirps, warbles, clucks, and cooing noises, often sounding more like a bird than a seal. When disturbed, it lifts its head to trill and thump, and observers report that when it does so, the long, soft palate expands for-

Half of all the seals in the world today are crabeater seals. These two (below) have hauled out onto a lava beach at Telephone Bay on Deception Island, but they are more frequently creatures of drifting pack ice.

ward to meet the base of the tongue, giving the distinct impression that the seal has two pink tennis balls at the back of its mouth.

Nothing is known of the Ross seal's breeding habits, and only one newborn Ross seal has ever been seen. It weighed 37 pounds (16.8 kg) and was a little over 3 feet (96.5 cm) long. Its coat was similar in color to the adult coat. Obviously just born—the afterbirth was not yet frozen—the pup squawked and squealed, crawled around on the ice, and swam over to the next floe in the thirty minutes that observers watched it. The pup was born in mid-November.

The adult seals molt in January, and they appear to fast at this time. When they eat, they eat mainly octopus and squid with some fish and krill thrown in for flavor. Their only enemy seems to be the leopard seal, but this is conjecture based on the scars seen on some Ross seals.

Worldwide population figures are largely guesses, but 100,000 to 150,000 are the numbers most frequently bruited about.

Crabeater Seal

(Lobodon carcinophagus)

Half of all the seals in the world are crabeater seals: their numbers are estimated at fifty million. There are as many crabeater seals in the world as all other species of seal combined. In spite of the huge numbers, very little is known about this species. These two circumstances—large population, little information—both derive from the same fact: the crabeater seal has never been hunted. Hunters need to know where and when to find their prey—no hunters, no information. The only other people likely to have any interest in the subject are research biologists who must wheedle grants from tight-fisted foundations in order to buy lots

© Marc Webber/EarthViews

of expensive equipment and get themselves down to Antarctica for the length of time necessary to collect such essential data as the number of whiskers that grow on either side of the crabeater's nose. To be awarded a grant they must show how this information contributes to the knowledge of man and the preservation of the planet. That's tough to do when the subject, with a population of fifty million, is not exactly endangered and does not offer even the slightest possibility of profit.

Crabeater seals vary in color from silver-gray to white; they are also known as the white seal. They are found on drifting pack ice and are seen in the greatest numbers in the Antarctic summer between January and March. They molt in January, mate in October, and the pups are born the following spring, in September and October. Crabeater seals form family groups, and the male defends and protects both mother and child

While all experts agree that the crabeater is the most populous seal on earth, the population estimates range from 15 million to 50 million. Nobody's actually counted noses. When Antarctic explorer Ernest Shackleton found a stowaway on his Imperial Trans-Antarctic Expedition, he went into a towering rage and gave the fellow a merciless tongue-lashing. He ended it by putting his face close to the cowering seal's and thundering, "If we run out of food and anyone has to be eaten, you will be first. Do you understand?" In fact, when the ill-fated expedition did come to grief, they survived on seal meat, much of it crabeater.

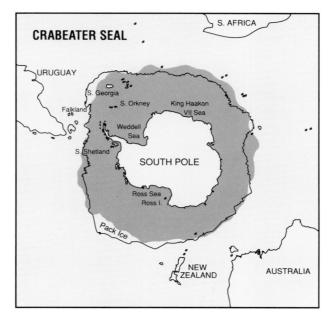

CRABEATER SEAL

S. AFRICA
URUGUAY
S. Georgia
Falkland
S. Orkney
King Haakon VII Sea
Weddell Sea
S. Shetland
SOUTH POLE
Ross Sea
Ross I.
Pack Ice
NEW ZEALAND
AUSTRALIA

With a head like a snake and a spotted half-ton body the leopard seal is easy to identify. One expert continued her description by remarking that ''at close quarters the large cheek teeth make identification certain.'' Since the leopard seal is the only seal reported to stalk and attack humans without provocation, perhaps close quarters inspections in the field are best avoided whenever possible.

from harm, which comes in the form of other males, leopard seals, or people. They make an angry hissing noise when disturbed and move swiftly and sinuously across the ice at speeds up to 15½ miles per hour (25 km).

Despite their name, crabeater seals do not eat crab. They eat large quantities of krill, sucking them in and squirting the water out through the sides of their mouth.

Their only predator is believed to be the leopard seal, since the parallel scars borne by many crabeater seals do not resemble the scars other seals receive from killer whales at all. On the other hand, the scars may be the consequence of a crabeater tribal rite, which, like the leopard seal attacks, has not yet been observed.

Leopard Seal

(Hydrurga leptonyx)

Leopard seals are the only seal known to attack people. Since the earliest days of antarctic exploration, there have been reports of leopard seals bursting from the water at the edge of the ice or sometimes through the ice itself and giving chase to an unwary explorer or scientist. A good example is Alfred Lansing's account taken from the diaries of the men on Sir Ernest Shackleton's Imperial Trans-Antarctic Expedition of 1915.

''Returning from a hunting trip, Orde-Lees, traveling on skis across the rotting surface of the ice had just about reached camp when an evil, knoblike head burst out of the water just in front of him. He turned and fled, pushing as hard as he could with his ski poles and shouting for Wild to bring his rifle.

''The animal—a sea leopard—sprang out of the water and came after him, bounding across the ice with the peculiar rocking-horse gait of a seal on land. The beast looked like a small dinosaur, with a long serpentine neck.

''After a half dozen leaps, the sea leopard had almost caught up with Orde-Lees when it unaccountably wheeled and plunged again into the water. By then, Orde-Lees had nearly reached the opposite side of the floe; he was about to cross to safe ice when the sea leopard's head exploded out of the water directly ahead of him. The animal had tracked his shadow across the ice. It made a savage lunge for Orde-Lees with its mouth open, revealing an enormous array of saw-like teeth. Orde-Lees' shouts for help rose to screams and he turned and raced away from his attacker.

''The animal leaped out of the water again in pursuit just as Wild arrived with his rifle. The sea leopard spotted Wild, and turned to attack him. Wild dropped to one knee and fired again and again at the onrushing beast. It was less than 30 feet away when it finally dropped.

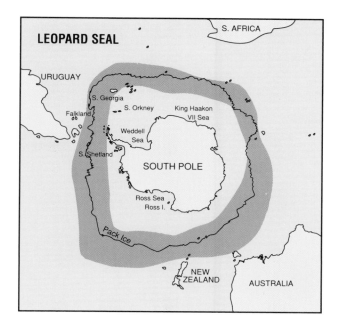

LEOPARD SEAL

"Two dog teams were required to bring the carcass into camp. It measured 12 feet long and they estimated its weight at about 1,100 pounds.''

Shackleton himself recorded the event in his diary: "One day a huge sea leopard climbed onto the floe and attacked one of the men, and Wild, hearing the shouting, ran out and shot it. When it was cut up we found several undigested fish in its stomach. These we fried in some blubber, and so had our only 'fresh' fish meal during the whole of our drift on the ice.''

Leopard seals, as is patently clear, are carnivores. They eat penguins by shaking them until the birds literally peel right out of their skin and they pick the bones clean. They attack young crabeater, Weddell, and elephant seals and the odd scientist. (They haven't eaten any scientists yet, but it's not for lack of trying.) They also eat fish, squid, octopus, and krill, sieving the krill through their teeth very much as the crabeater seal does. Fifty percent of their diet is krill.

Leopard seals take their name from their coat, which is spotted like a leopard's. They are dark gray on the back, light gray on the stomach, and have black and gray spots on the throat, shoulders, and sides. The head is large in proportion to the body, and the mouth opens unusually wide. It has a distinctly reptilian look about it.

Little is known about the breeding habits. Pups are believed to be born between September and January, an exceptionally long season in the Antarctic. The pups are dark gray with a nearly black stripe down the back. Researchers estimate that the pups nurse for four weeks and that the females mate after that. Males mature between three and six years, females at five. The adults molt any time between January and June.

Crabeater seals are often seen in family groups—a male, female, and pup—but the male is more likely to be a candidate to be the father of next year's pup than the father of the little one present. Still, he does his duty by defending mother and child against all comers, including other crabeater suitors, leopard seals, and people.

Leopard seals sometimes sing in their sleep. As out of character as it may seem, they are reported to make musical sighing sounds and to chirp, croon, and whistle. They also gargle, grunt, and sound a guttural alarm by vibrating their tongue as air is expelled through the mouth, producing a noise very like a Bronx cheer.

The leopard seal's only natural enemy is probably the killer whale. There are an estimated 250,000 to 800,000 leopard seals in the world.

Southern Elephant Seal

(Mirounga leonina)

The southern elephant seal is the largest pinniped in the world. It is larger than its cousin, the northern elephant seal, by a ton (0.9 metric tons) or more in weight, though by only 18 inches (45 cm) in length. Males are 16½ feet (5 m) long and three to four times the size of the females, who are dainty by comparison. The males weigh 7,200 pounds (3.7 metric tons), the females a mere 1,980 pounds (900 kg).

They are circumpolar and found on most of the subantarctic islands. Stragglers occasionally stray to South Africa, aided by the west wind drift, or to New Zealand and Australia. The longest known journey of an elephant seal was made by a pup tagged on South Georgia Island when it was three weeks old and found fourteen months later on the South African coast. Since pups stay at the rookery for three to four months, it had wandered nearly 3,000 miles (4,800 km) in less than a year!

The southern elephant seal's distinguishing feature is its gargantuan nose. Had Cyrano de Bergerac ever seen a southern elephant seal, he would never have given his own nose another thought. The appendage

By far the largest seal in the world, Southern elephant seal males weigh 1,000 pounds (454 kg) more than the next largest species of seal, their Pacific cousin, the Northern elephant seal. The Latin name *Mirounga* is derived from Miouroung, the Australian native word for the Elephant Seal. *Leonina* is Latin for lion-like, describing both the male's impressive size and the equally impressive roar.

© Mark E. Gibson

oth species of elephant seal, the northern elephant seal (*Mirounga angustrostris,* above) and the southern elephant seal (*M. leonina*) are related by fossil evidence to the monk seals (Monachine). Scientists believe that this ancient ancestor passed through the Caribbean to the Pacific to give rise to the northern elephant seal while others of its kin took a left turn and headed south along the Pacific coast of South America to give rise to the southern elephant seal.

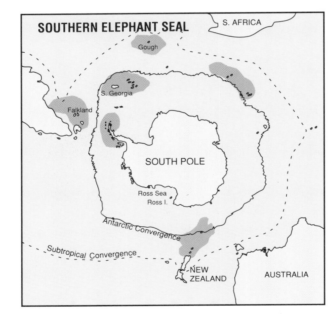

SOUTHERN ELEPHANT SEAL

S. AFRICA
Gough
S. Georgia
Falkland
SOUTH POLE
Ross Sea
Ross I.
Antarctic Convergence
Subtropical Convergence
NEW ZEALAND
AUSTRALIA

appears to work as a personal public address system, amplifying the roar of the bull, which can be heard as much as two miles away. Females never develop the enlarged proboscis, though one authority reports that ''occasional individuals may be able to pucker the snout a little.''

It takes eight years for the nose, which is really an enlargement of the nasal cavity like the hooded seal's, to reach its full glory, with the tip hanging down over the mouth so that it can be blown up like a balloon to look like a large round bolster atop the snout. Its primary function appears to be to make big bulls look even bigger and to am-

plify the bull's roars to frighten off other males during the breeding season.

Like northern elephant seals, southern elephant seals breed in harems. The biggest, noisiest bulls collect harems ranging from twenty to forty females, though occasionally harems can get up to one hundred. The females haul out on the island beaches to pup in September, and the pups are born about a week later, most of them in October. Pups nurse for three weeks, gaining as much as 20 pounds (9 kg) per day. Their mothers lose more than 700 pounds (320 kg) in these three weeks. The pups weigh 75 to 100 pounds (35–45 kg) at birth and 310 to 400 pounds (140–180 kg) at weaning, a gain of 300 pounds (138 kg) in three weeks, or 100 pounds (46 kg) per week!

While the mothers nurse, the males fight with each other for territory and dominance. Battling males represent the greatest danger not to each other but to the pups. Heedless of the impact of seven tons of rampaging bull galumphing over a youngster, the males brook no interference in their pursuit of status. The little ones often do not survive the experience. Nearly 50 percent of the pups do not live through their first year.

The cows mate soon after the pup is weaned. The blastocyst is held for four months before implanting itself in March. Both males and females fast during breeding for about a month. After mating, the females return to the sea to feed, and by November, the males have returned to the sea as well.

Females are brown, the males a dark gray after molting that turns a reddish brown over the year. Males have a chest shield of rough, thick, corrugated skin, often heavily scarred from fighting. Their fights consist mostly of roaring, pushing, and shoving. They seldom wound each other seriously and never fight to the death. Bulls live as long as twenty years. Cows live about twelve years and produce seven pups in their lifetime.

Pups molt before they leave the rookery. Molting is an itchy, irritating process, and wherever the ground is not frozen, the pups wriggle themselves into muddy wallows to soothe their skin. Southern elephant seals have little hair, and what hair they have is short, rough, and stiff. They shed skin and hair together, the old skin falling off in big, ragged patches, giving the animals a decidedly mangy look. They molt in the antarctic summer months, the younger seals first and then in relays by age group, starting in December with the youngest and ending with the breeding bulls in March. (Seasons on the southern hemisphere are opposite of those in the northern hemisphere, making December summer and July winter.)

The seals maintain their body temperature, not with a dense underfur, but with a

T he peculiar snout that gives the elephant seal its name is found only on adult males, and it takes about eight years to develop to its full glory. No one knows exactly what its purpose is in the greater scheme of things, but it seems to function as an amplifier for the bull's roar so that he can be heard for miles.

© Wolfgang Kaehler

Northern elephant seals and Hawaiian monk seals (below) share the distinction of living in warm climates year round. When temperatures are high they do as little as possible.

thick layer of blubber. This blubber renders an edible oil, and when the sealers had nearly exterminated the antarctic fur seals, they started in on the southern elephant seals for their oil. Between 1820 and 1900, they pursued the seals so relentlessly that there was virtually nothing left to hunt by the end of the century. By 1910, the herds had recovered, and sealing was once more big business. In the next fifty years, more than 259,000 were killed. Today the southern elephant seal is fully protected, but it is not clear whether the herds have been able to rebuild themselves. The waters of the Antarctic are heavily fished, and there is a serious possibility that their recovery may be hampered by lack of food.

Northern Elephant Seal

(Mirounga angustirostris)

© Dan Polin

The Northern elephant seal is one of the greatest ecological comeback stories in the world. Reduced at the end of the nineteenth century to possibly as few as twenty by sealers, the population now numbers over 100,000. This miraculous recovery was achieved by the simple expedient of banning the seal hunt. The first protective laws were passed by Mexico as early as 1911, reinforced by even stricter laws in 1922, and as the animals expanded their range north along the Pacific coast, they were further protected by the United States under the Marine Mammal Act. As the population continues to expand its range into its traditional feeding and breeding grounds, it is hoped that Canada will see its way clear to protecting the Northern elephant seals as they feed along the coast of British Columbia.

Northern elephant seals, while smaller than the Southern elephant seals in Antarctica, are, nonetheless, the largest pinnipeds north of the Equator. Adult males weigh more than 1,000 pounds (455 kg), less than Southern elephant seal males, but adult females are about the same size as their southern cousins. The males weigh three tons (2.7 metric tons), the females, only a ton (.9 metric tons). Males range in length from 15 to 18 feet (4.5 to 5.5 m), the females from 9 to 12 feet (2.7 to 4 m).

Northern elephant seals breed on islands off the west coast of North America from Mexico to northern California, and on beaches on the California mainland at Big Sur, Ano Nuevo, and Point Reyes. Pups are born in the winter, between December and February. Females haul out for approximately a month to give birth, nurse, and mate, before heading back out to sea.

Northern elephant seals are the largest seals in the northern hemisphere. The males weigh three tons (2.7 metric tons). The females are dainty by comparison, weighing a mere ton (.9 metric tons). Huge as they are, they were easy prey for sealers. They are slow, predictable, and unafraid of people. Forty years of sealing brought them to the edge of extinction.

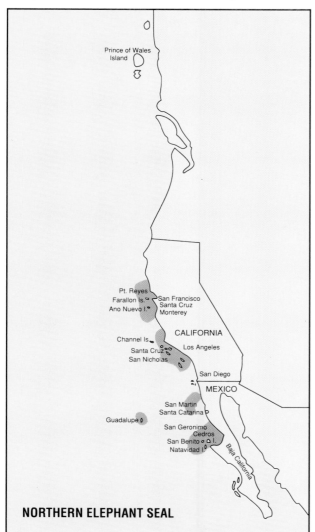

Prince of Wales Island

Pt. Reyes
Farallon Is
Ano Nuevo I.
San Francisco
Santa Cruz
Monterey
CALIFORNIA
Channel Is.
Santa Cruz
San Nicholas
Los Angeles
San Diego
MEXICO
San Martin
Santa Catarina I.
Guadalupe I.
San Geronimo
Cedros
San Benito I.
Natavidad I.
Baja California

NORTHERN ELEPHANT SEAL

They do not feed during the breeding season, nor during the molt which takes place between May and June. Adult males molt during July and August. Molting is reported to look bad and smell worse. Elephant seals have no fur, so they molt the surface layers of their skin which fall off in large, ragged patches, leaving more than one ill-informed observer to conclude that the molting seals have some horrible disease. The new coat is a clean silvery grey on males, a fresh brown on females.

Elephant seal pups are nearly 5 feet long (1.5 m) and weigh approximately 100 pounds (46 kg) at birth. There are records of pups weighing 600 pounds (272 kg) at weaning, but most weigh somewhat less. Still, the pups normally gain between 400 and 500 pounds (173 to 227 kg) in four weeks of nursing. They fast for two to three months after weaning, gathering in small groups called "weaner pods". They learn to swim by themselves, taking about a week to master the art. It takes them another six weeks to learn to dive and stay underwater for 10 to 15 minutes. By May, most of the weaned pups have headed north along the coast to

© Gerry Ellis/Ellis Wildlife Collection

the summer feeding grounds. Fifteen percent of them will not survive their first year. Nearly 50 percent of the females and 85 percent of the male elephant seals do not survive to breeding age, which is four years for females and eight years for males. They are preyed upon by both the great white sharks and killer whales.

Northern elephant seals eat squid and bottom fish. They hold the record for diving deeper than any other known seal: 4,125 feet (1,250 m), more than three-quarters of a mile (1.3 km) down, before the female being measured got irritated and rubbed the time/depth recording device off her back.

© Frank S. Balthis/Nature's Design   (opposite page) © Gerry Ellis/Ellis Wildlife Collection

Bull elephant seals (far left) battle for territorial rights by galumphing at each other as fast as they can and plowing into each other with a resounding crash. Bulls have thick, heavily calloused chest shields which protect them from their rivals' slashing canines. Some blood may be drawn, but most fights end without serious damage.

Lacking fur, elephant seals (above) molt the top layers of skin. It is reportedly a vile smelling process, and looks decidedly mangy. Worse yet, from the seals' point of view, it itches like crazy.

Northern elephant seal pups (left) are weaned when their mothers return to the sea to feed, about a month after birth. In that month, they gain about 100 pounds (45 kg) a week. They learn to swim, feed, and migrate by themselves.

Chapter Three

Sea Lions and Fur Seals

Sea lions and fur seals belong to the family *Otariidae*, which means "little eared," and a careful observer will see that their ears are very little indeed, no more than 2½ (6 cm) inches long. Sea lions are classed in the subfamily *Otariinae,* referring again to their ears, and the fur seals are classified as *Arctocephalinae,* which means "bear head." Until this century, fur seals were called sea bears.

The other major differences between the otarids and the phocids are that sea lions and fur seals are found only in the sea, never in bays or fresh water. Their hind flippers can be turned forward to function like little feet so that they appear to walk on land, rather than hump and lurch along as the true seals do. They have no hair on the palms or the soles of their flippers, and their first three "fingers" have longer nails than the last two. Their skin is light-colored under their fur, and all females have four nipples.

There are five species of sea lions and ten species of fur seals.

A portrait of a female Australian sea lion, one of the *Otarids,* or "eared seals". The little ear that gives the *Otarids* their name is clearly visible.

SEA LIONS

Steller's Sea Lion

(Eumetopias jubatus)

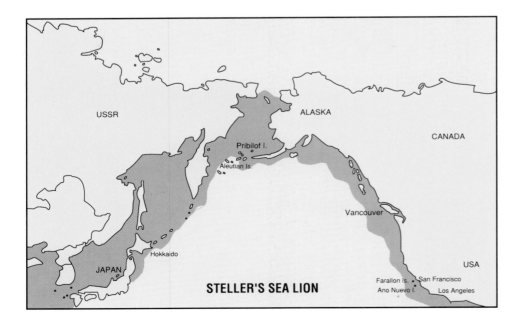

Note: The gray area in each map indicates the seal's range.

Largest of the sea lions, Steller's sea lion is also the most lionlike, at least in appearance. Its size, tawny color, and the male's bristling mane all contribute to make the name particularly apt. Bulls are more than three times the size of the cows, weighing 2,000 pounds (907 kg) to the females' 600 pounds (270 kg).

Steller's sea lions range from the Arctic down both sides of the Pacific, from the Pribilofs to Hokkaido in the east and Ano Nuevo Island in the west. They breed on rocky little islands and open sea coasts.

Pups are born in mid-June, and they nurse for at least a year, and sometimes for more than three. A cow may nurse both her new pup *and* her pup from the previous year. They are active mothers, sometimes acting as their own midwives by tugging gently at the pup with their teeth as it is born.

The pups do little but sleep and nurse their first few days. Their mothers are relaxed and calm while the little one nurses, but when it stops, they pick it up, squeal at it, and check it out from every angle. The pups stay close to the mothers for the first few weeks, but then they form their own groups and play and sleep together. They have mock battles and splash about in tidepools but steer clear of the ocean. They are nearly two months old before they venture into even protected waters.

The males form one herd, and the females and young another. Most of the bulls arrive in May, mate by the end of August (Steller's sea lions mate on land), and head back out to sea. It is reported that the bulls make a sound reminiscent of a moped a block away. They ignore the pups entirely. Cows have their first pups when they're five years old; males mature between three and eight years.

All sea lions form "rafts," floating together in the water and drifting along in groups of several hundred. They may all dive simultaneously, though why or how the signal is given, no one knows.

Steller's sea lions eat squid and many different kinds of fish: herring, halibut, flounder, sculpin, pollack, cod, lampreys, and salmon. Despite the bitter complaints of salmon fishermen, the research shows that the amount of salmon eaten by both sea lions and harbor seals in British Columbia amounts to a negligible 2.5 percent of the commercial catch. Sea lions observed feeding at the mouth of the Rogue River in Oregon ate 87 percent lampreys and 2 percent salmon—the other 11 percent was no longer identifiable. Since lamprey eels are parasites on salmon, sea lions may actually increase the numbers of salmon by eating huge numbers of their parasites. The fishermen's revenge of surreptitiously shooting sea lions may well create precisely the situation they fear the most: fewer and fewer salmon. Stel-

© Frank S. Balthis/Nature's Design

ler's sea lions also occasionally eat young ringed seals, northern fur seals, and sea otters.

Most seals that live in American waters have increased in numbers since they were granted full protection under the Marine Mammal Act in 1972. Steller's sea lions are the sole exception to that rule. A startling decline of 50 percent in the reproduction rate has occurred at the breeding grounds in the eastern Aleutian Islands, but precisely why is still unknown. The total population in 1960 was estimated at between 240,000 and 300,000, but that does not take into account the reproductive failure observed since 1977, nor the devastating damage to their feeding and breeding grounds caused by the Exxon oil spill in Prince William Sound off the Alaska coast.

Oceanic Society Expeditions offers tours to see Steller's sea lions in southeast Alaska and on the Farallon Islands off California. (Call 415-441-1106 for southeast Alaska tours, 415-474-3385 for day trips to the Farallons.)

California Sea Lion

(Zalophus californianus)

This is the one seal everybody knows, the star of the circus, the clown of the zoo. Extraordinarily intelligent and stupendously well coordinated, California sea lions can perform feats of balance that virtually no other animal could even attempt. Trained, they can climb steps, swim across a pond,

There are more California sea lions on Ano Nuevo Island than any of the other three species of seals that use the island for their rookeries—Northern elephant seals, Steller sea lions, and Pacific harbor seals. They are also the only seals that don't breed on the island.

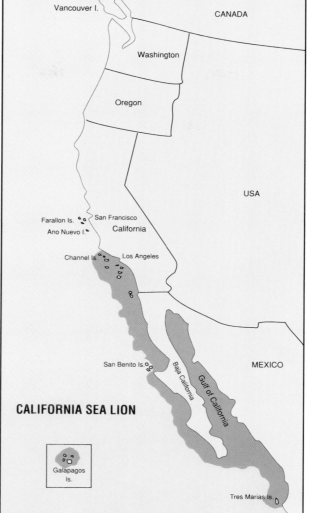

CALIFORNIA SEA LION

© Frank S. Balthis/Nature's Design

California sea lions love to play. They practically invented body surfing, and I have often envied their speed and grace and daring at riding the crest of a wave. California sea lions often "raft" together, dozens at a time, lazing in the water, until some subtle, mysterious signal is given, and they all dive instantly.

and climb back out again, all while balancing a wineglass full of water on their nose, and never spill a drop. In teams, they toss balls from nose to nose while perched on stools and never miss a bounce—the sea lion version of the Harlem Globetrotters. Having carried it off, they may well give themselves a well-deserved round of applause by clapping their foreflippers enthusiastically.

Left to their own devices in the wild, they body surf California's waves, blow bubbles and then catch them, play tag, chase one another, and turn underwater somersaults for the sheer, exuberant fun of it. All seals are playful, but the California sea lion may well be the most playful of all.

Despite their name, California sea lions are also found in Japan and in the Galapagos Islands. (The Japanese sea lions lived on an island ceded to Korea after World War II, and since then there have been no further reports of them.) They are found on Pacific sea coasts and islands from Vancouver Island, British Columbia, to Islas Tres Marias in Mexico. A shore-living seal, it seldom strays more than 10 miles (16 km) from land.

California sea lions are a rich chocolate brown. Males have an exceptionally high forehead called a sagittal crest, which may

A sub-species of the California sea lion, sometimes called the Galapagos sea lion (above), is found on the Galapagos Islands, a series of tiny volcanic islands on the Equator 600 miles (960 km) west of Ecuador. Utterly unafraid of people, the sea lions scarcely looked up as I and my fellow adventurers walked among them, photographing. The Islands have been designated a nature reserve and both plants and animals are strictly protected.

be quite a bit lighter. Bulls are three times the size of cows, weighing nearly 660 pounds (300 kg) to the females' 220 (100 kg).

The cows and young seals stay at the breeding grounds year-round or migrate south. Only the adult males are found much north of Ano Nuevo Island in California. Bulls stake a claim on a piece of breeding territory near the water for about two weeks, during which time they patrol up and down and bark unceasingly. California sea lions are notable for their propensity to bark night and day.

After two weeks the males go to sea to feed. When they come back, they start all over again, establishing a new territory. These territorial boundaries are observed only by the adult males; the females ignore them entirely, simply going about the business of bearing and nursing pups amidst the barking and bellicosity of the males. If the females decide to move, the bulls pull up stakes and follow them.

Pups are born in June on the Channel Islands and weigh about 13½ pounds (6 kg). California sea lions are conscientious mothers for the first two or three days, taking the pups everywhere they go and never letting them out of their reach. When the mother

needs to cool off, she hauls the little one, often kicking and screaming, into the water with her to keep it within reach. This has led to the pretty story that sea lions teach their babies to swim, but in fact the pups learn by themselves, generally not until they are at least a couple of months old. Pups nurse until the next pup is born, ordinarily about a year. After a week under the mothers' watchful eyes, the pups gather in their own groups, to sleep, play, and explore together.

The females approach the bulls for mating by rubbing up against them and flirting in a manner that can only be described as sweetly demure. They also end the session by pulling away and biting the male. They mate about two weeks after the pups are born.

California sea lions eat mostly squid and octopus, along with fish such as hake, herring, and anchovies. Because they are found in areas where salmon are fished commercially, they are not popular with salmon fishermen, but California sea lions actually prefer squid to salmon. Like Steller's sea lions, they eat huge numbers of lamprey eels, which parasitize salmon. California sea lions may well contribute more to increasing the salmon population than decreasing it.

© Frank S. Balthis/Nature's Design

The worldwide population of California sea lions is estimated at 99,000; 20,000 to 50,000 of these are found in the Galapagos Islands.

California sea lions can be seen many places along the West Coast, including Seal Caves in Oregon, Seal Rocks in San Francisco (you can eat at the Cliff House and watch them), the Farallon Islands, and San Benito Island in Baja California, where you can actually play with them. Oceanic Society Expeditions offers tours to the Farallons and San Benito. (Call 415-441-1106 for Baja, 415-474-3385 for the Farallon Islands.) You can swim with the California sea lions in the Galapagos Islands. Overseas Adventure Tours in Cambridge, Massachusetts can get you there. (Call 800-221-0814.)

Southern Sea Lion

(Otaria byronia)

"Sea-wolves of many colors" were reported on the coasts of South America in 1520 in Pigafetta's account of Magellan's circumnavigation of the globe. Southern sea lions are still found from Isla Lobos del Tierra off northern Peru in the Pacific around Cape

Horn to Lobos Island off the coast of Uruguay in the Atlantic.

Because we are land mammals, we tend to think in terrestrial terms when naming creatures of the sea. Hence, seals have been variously identified as sea lions, sea bears, and sea wolves. The golden age of Spanish exploration left us with innumerable islands and inlets containing the word *lobos*, which properly means wolf but which Spanish sailors used to identify seals.

Southern sea lions are also lionlike in looks. The males have a huge, heavy head, a pug nose, and an immense tawny mane. Their color varies from dark brown to reddish brown to yellow. Typically, the body is very dark and the head and neck quite blond—and the effect is rather like a sea-going centaur with the head of a lion and the body of a seal. Pups are black at birth.

SOUTHERN SEA LION

Bulls are more than twice the size of cows, weighing about 660 pounds (300 kg) to the females' 318 pounds (144 kg). The herd ordinarily consists of all ages and sexes together in a single group, except during breeding when the young males and idle bulls hang around on the edges devising mischief. Each rookery has several harems, but they are often so closely packed that only the breeding bulls, who worry about these things, know where one ends and the next begins. The breeding bull will defend his territory valiantly from idle bulls and stays faithfully at his chosen post, even when high tide nearly inundates him. Sometimes the idle bulls gang up on a harem bull, attacking him and stealing the cows and pups in his harem. About nine cows constitute a respectable harem.

Cows mate a few days after birthing, after which the males allow them to return to the

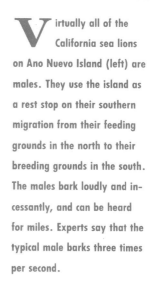

Virtually all of the California sea lions on Ano Nuevo Island (left) are males. They use the island as a rest stop on their southern migration from their feeding grounds in the north to their breeding grounds in the south. The males bark loudly and incessantly, and can be heard for miles. Experts say that the typical male barks three times per second.

Southern sea lion bulls are more than twice the size of the cows (above). They have a blonde mane on a brunette body, a huge head, a thick, muscular neck, and an upturned snout. The cows are sleek and slim by comparison. Killer whales attack the rookeries at Peninsula Valdes, Argentina; one is said to have flipped a full grown sea lion twenty feet (6 m) in the air with its flukes.

Australian seal lion bulls (far right) are a dark chocolate color, while females are silver-gray on top and cream-colored on the belly.

sea to feed. The pups nurse until the birth of the next pup the following year. Most pups are born between Christmas and New Year's Day.

Altogether the bulls spend two months without food or much sleep, wearing themselves out with fighting and sex. By February, they are thin and exhausted and must spend the next six months eating and sleeping to recover their strength so they can do it again.

Pups collect into pup pods, playing and sleeping, but do not go near the water without much persuasion from their mothers. They are afraid of deep water and will climb on their mothers' backs sooner than swim.

The male southern sea lion matures at six, when the mane begins to appear, the female at five, when she produces her first pup. They molt any time between April and August.

They eat squid and small crustaceans, gentoo, rockhopper and Magellanic penguins, and South American fur seals. They also eat stones, as most seals do, and up to 20 pounds (9 kg) of little sharp rocks have been found in their stomachs.

Only killer whales, leopard seals, and people are serious predators of the southern sea lion. There has been a shocking reduction in numbers over the last twenty years—from 400,000 to 30,000 in the Falklands alone—and the worldwide population is estimated

now at 240,000. In Uruguay, fishermen kill them in great numbers, and the government kills a certain number in its commercial sealing operations.

They are protected in Argentina, Peru, and Chile. In Puerto Madryn, in Chubut, Argentina, more than 400,000 tourists a year visit the seal rookeries to see southern sea lions and South American fur seals—more tourists than there are sea lions!

Australian Sea Lion

(Neophoca cinerea)

Its Latin name is as simply descriptive as one might hope: it means ''ash-colored new seal'' because that's what the Australian sea lion looked like to François Peron when he

© Gerry Ellis/Ellis Wildlife Collection

Australian sea lions (right) are "eared seals", classified as *Otarids*. The small, scroll-shaped ear is clearly visible as this youngster takes its afternoon nap.

first saw them on Kangaroo Island in the early 1800s. He described them and published their eminently sensible scientific name in 1816. Today tourists can go to Kangaroo Island, off the coast of Australia near Adelaide, to watch Peron's grayish "new seal."

Perhaps one of those curious tourists will make the observation that unlocks the mystery of the Australian sea lion's breeding habits. Unlike any other seal, Australian sea lion pups are not born at the same time every year, but instead may be born at any time during the year. Some of the research suggests that pups are born every eighteen months, yet the cows were observed to mate within a week or so of giving birth. That means either that pregnancy lasts an exceptionally long fourteen months or the blastocyst is carried for as long as nine or ten

© John Cancalosi/Tom Stack & Associates

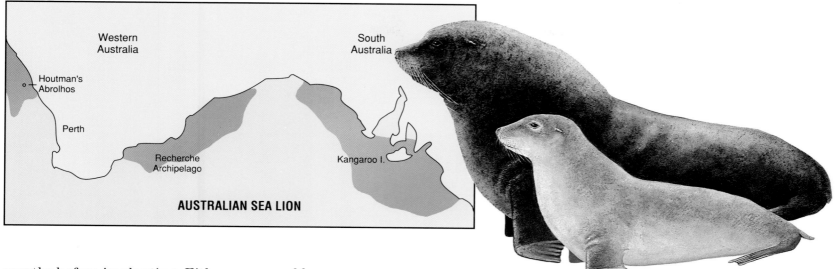

months before implanting. Either case would be highly unusual among pinnipeds, but no one really knows, except, presumably, the mother seal.

Males are nearly four times the size of females, and they take advantage of this difference in size to actively herd the females in their harems. In spite of the mothers' delicate condition, the bulls are, to quote one authority, "quite ruthless in this, and can be very rough with the cows." The cows haul out three days before the pup is born. Like other sea lions, the pups nurse for about a year. The Australian sea lion is an attentive mother for the first two weeks, never leaving the pup's side, whether it is nursing, sleeping, or scrambling all over her. The pup does not begin to venture into the water before it is three months old.

The big bulls are no gentler with the pups than with the mothers—as a species, Australian sea lions are aggressive—and pups are frequently bitten or shaken severely and tossed aside. The young males and adult females also feel free to pick on the little guys, even when the pups are sleeping or quietly minding their own business.

Females are silver-gray on top, cream-colored on the belly. Bulls are the color of bitter chocolate, with a white streak from the top of the head to the nape of the neck. Males go through a series of color changes as they age, getting progressively darker on the body, progressively lighter at the top of the head. Males have longer, coarser hair on the mane and massive shoulders.

Australian sea lions eat fish and squid and have been seen tearing out the livers of sharks caught in nets. They are preyed upon, in turn, by white pointer sharks, which grow to record sizes off Dangerous Reef. The Australian sea lion is protected in Australia, though fishermen kill some. There are believed to be 5,000 Australian sea lions.

Hooker's Sea Lion

(Phocarctos hookeri)

Hooker's sea lions are much gentler than the Australian sea lions. Bulls line the waterfront where the pregnant cows haul out, but they are seldom successful in capturing a cow. For the most part, the cows haul out together, lying in great heaps on the beach. Bulls put on a ritualized territorial display, but they do not herd the cows or interfere with them in any way. What the bulls defend is not a harem so much as a circle of personal space 6 feet (2 m) in diameter. They defend this space, even when they have no females at all, but it is largely a ceremonial act, and serious fights are rare. They do not eat during the two months of the breeding season or even take a quick dip to cool off.

The breeding season starts in December, and pups are born through the first week in January. Huge flocks of skuas eat the afterbirth, as seagulls do with northern elephant seals. Pups nurse within a half-hour of being born and continue to nurse for a year. Sleeping cows often waken to find a little stranger

Body pulled up to its full height, head thrown back, and mouth wide open are all threat gestures (far left). Ordinarily, a threat stance is sufficient to persuade one seal or the other to withdraw. Even when fights ensue, they are never fights to the death. A sign of submission is all that's required to end most disputes, and then both parties go on about their business.

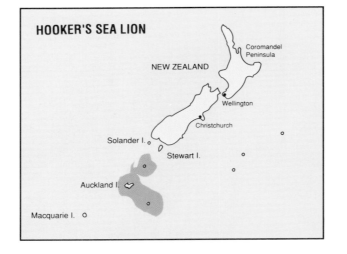

HOOKER'S SEA LION

Sea lions on the grass? That's the case with these Hooker's sea lions on Enderby Island south of New Zealand. The weather is so fierce there that the sea lions seek shelter from driving wind and rain among the bushes.

nursing alongside their own pup—the pup's version, one supposes, of having a playmate over for dinner. The mothers generally do not put up with this, but pups still make the rounds of sleeping cows in the hope of picking up an extra meal. They are much more active than Australian sea lion pups and are strong swimmers by the time they are two months old. Cows mate about a week after birth.

Perhaps the oddest thing about Hooker's sea lions is that they can be found deep in the forest on Enderby Island, where they find shelter against the raging winds and driving rains that are typical of the Auckland Islands.

The Auckland Islands, of which Enderby is one, proved inhospitable, despite several attempts at human colonization, so domesticated animals—cattle, sheep, goats, pigs, and rabbits—were released in the hope that they might one day provide food for any sailors who survived the many shipwrecks of these treacherous waters. The rabbits dig burrows, as rabbits do, and on occasion pups wriggle into them to escape the wild winds and rain. If, as sometimes happens, they can't get out again, they starve.

Bulls are black, with the requisite mane, and females look almost exactly like Australian sea lions, silver-gray on top, creamy on the bottom. They eat penguins, squid, crab, shrimp, and crayfish, and, like so many other seals, stones. The Auckland Islands, 200 miles (322 km) south of New Zealand, became a sealing center in 1822, and the seals were virtually wiped out within eight years. Under an exceptionally enlightened wildlife policy, both sea lions and fur seals have been fully protected since 1881. The Aucklands are today a wildlife and wildflower reserve, as well as a shipwrecked sailor's best hope for survival.

FUR SEALS

Guadalupe Fur Seal

(Arctocephalus townsendii)

Very little is known about the Guadalupe fur seal. Discovered by Russian sealers in about 1800, they were virtually exterminated by 1820. In 1892, Dr. Charles H. Townsend brought four skulls back for the Museum of Natural History in New York, but no one knew what the seal looked like until 1928, when Mexican fishermen captured two bulls that were sent to the San Diego Zoo. At that time, the fishermen estimated there were perhaps sixty seals on Guadalupe Island.

Guadalupe fur seals breed on the lava rock beaches at the base of high cliffs and in the caves on the east side of Guadalupe Island off the Pacific Coast of Baja California. They penetrate deeply into the caves, at least 85 feet (25 m). There were once so many that their bodies wore the rough lava as smooth and polished as glass. Bulls arrive in May and choose their territories. Harems consist of about ten cows, and the black-coated pups are born in June.

The adults are a dark, grizzled brown and have long, pointed noses. Males are about 6 feet (1.8 m) long and weigh about 300 pounds (136 kg); females probably weigh less than 100 pounds (45 kg), but none have ever been measured and weighed. They are reported to roar, bark, and cough.

Tourists may see both the Guadalupe fur seal and northern elephant seal on Guadalupe Island through Oceanic Society Expedi-

Guadalupe fur seals can be distinguished from other fur seals by their very long, very pointed noses, and are found on the lava beaches on the east coast of Guadalupe Island off the coast of Baja California. They prefer to breed in coastal caves, going as deep as seventy-five feet (23 m) into the caves to give birth. They are reported to make three sounds, a cough, a bark, and a roar, depending, of course, on the situation.

© D. Cavagnaro

Galapagos fur seals, found only in the Galapagos Islands, are the smallest of the fur seals. The males are barely five feet (1.5 m) long, the females slightly smaller. While visiting the islands, I saw them curled up, asleep, in the niches of a rocky grotto high above the water.

tions (Fort Mason Center, Building E, San Francisco, California 94123, 415-441-1106). Guadalupe fur seals are fully protected in both Mexican and American waters—they sometimes reach the Channel Islands off the California coast at Santa Barbara—and the total population is estimated at between 500 and 1,000 seals.

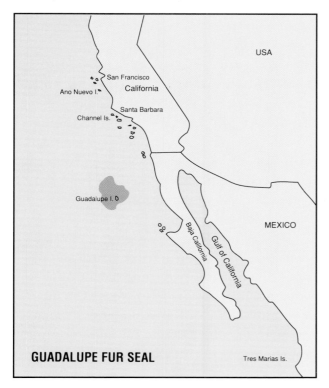

GUADALUPE FUR SEAL

Galapagos Fur Seal

(Arctocephalus galapagoensis)

The smallest of all the fur seals, the Galapagos fur seal male is only about 5 feet (15 m) long, the female even smaller. They are grayish brown on the back with light tan heads and ears, and they have a little button nose.

The Galapagos fur seal is found on at least ten of the Galapagos Islands. Beyond the fact that newborn pups have been seen in August and pups of all ages in December, almost nothing is known about their breeding. They are found in caves and on rocky

I swam with a Galapagos fur seal in a little grotto near James Bay, Santiago Island. It sped toward my face mask, turning aside only inches from my face. It examined me from all angles, swimming upside down to investigate me from underneath, leaving a trail of silver bubbles to show where it had been. Convinced after a half hour of playing together that it would not hurt me, I extended my hand. The first time it came close, but didn't touch me; the second time, it brushed my hand with its whiskers. That one moment was worth traveling thousands of miles from home.

© Craig McLean

beaches. They share the Galapagos with California sea lions, but as the sea lions like sandy beaches and the fur seals rocky shores, the two coexist peaceably.

Nothing is reported on either their prey or their predators. Humans have been their most devastating predator, and nineteenth-century sealing all but wiped them from the face of the earth. Today, they are fully protected, and their population numbers around 1,000.

Overseas Adventure Travel of Cambridge, Massachusetts, offers a trip to the Galapagos Islands by private yacht, and a chance to swim and play with the fur seals in small pools at the base of the lava cliffs on James Island. (Call 800-221-0814 for more information about this exciting trip.)

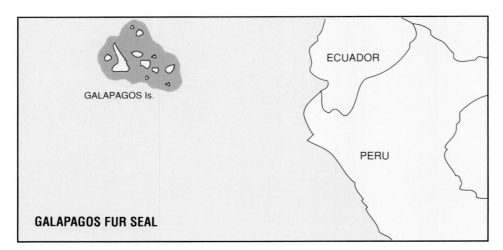

GALAPAGOS Is.

ECUADOR

PERU

GALAPAGOS FUR SEAL

© J. Francis

The English adventurer William Dampier saw Juan Fernandez fur seals in 1683. In his *New Voyage Round the World* he wrote, "Seals swim as thick as if they had no other place in the world to live. Not a bay or rock is not full of them. The seals at Juan Fernandez have a fine, thick, short fur, the like of which I have not taken notice of anywhere but in these seas. There are always thousands—I might say possibly millions—coming and going around the island, which is covered with them for a mile or two from shore."

Juan Fernandez Fur Seal

(Arctocephalus philippii)

Beyond the fact that there were millions of fur seals on the Juan Fernandez Islands when they were discovered in 1683 and only two hundred could be found in 1965, little is known of the Juan Fernandez fur seal. It is a gentle creature, about 6½ feet (2 m) long, weighing approximately 350 pounds (159 kg). They are very dark brown and have a sharply pointed nose. The males have a thick, silvery mane. Pups are born in December.

Like the Guadalupe fur seal, the Juan Fernandez fur seal hauls out on lava rocks below steep cliffs and in sea caves. Both seals reportedly like to hang upside down in the water, leaving only their hind flippers to be seen swaying gently at the surface. These are the "sea lions" Alexander Selkirk heard roaring by the hundreds when he was marooned on Isla Mas á Tierra (Isla Robinson Crusoe). Selkirk's story of life on a desert island inspired Daniel Defoe to write the fictionalized version, the famous *Robinson Crusoe.*

JUAN FERNANDEZ FUR SEAL

Juan Fernandez Is.

BRAZIL

ARGENTINA

CHILE

URUGUAY

Atlantic Ocean

South American Fur Seal

(Arctocephalus australis)

South American fur seal pups are born in November and stay with their mother about a year. Cows mate a week after birth. No harems are formed, but breeding bulls do establish and defend territories. They battle other males for the right to mate—females apparently are not consulted on the subject —and the young or defeated males hang out on the beach close to the water, not doing much except just messing around. The herd heads back out to sea at the beginning of the new year.

South American fur seals are substantially smaller than southern sea lions, with which they share much of their range along both coasts of South America. Male fur seals are over 6 feet (1.9 m) long and weigh 350 pounds (159 kg); the females are not quite 5 feet (1.4 m) long and weigh only 106 pounds (48 kg). Adult males are a grizzled black, but all the others are various shades of dark— black, gray, brown—on the back and paler on the stomach.

SOUTH AMERICAN FUR SEAL

The fur seals eat squid, shrimp, sea snails, and fish. They are eaten by killer whales, sharks, and South American sea lions and killed by sealers.

Tourists may visit the seal rookeries of Argentina to see both the South American fur seal and the southern sea lion in Puerto Madryn, Chubut Province. More than 400,000 tourists go every year to see these fascinating creatures of two worlds, the land and the sea. Sealers in Uruguay still hunt the South American fur seal. The hunt takes place in the winter in July and August (in the southern hemisphere the seasons are reversed), and the government takes about 12,000 seals a year for their oil and skins. The worldwide population is estimated at 320,000 seals.

Subantarctic Fur Seal

(Arctocephalus tropicalis)

Subantarctic fur seals are very easy to spot, just in case you ever run across one: the body is dark gray-brown, the face and chest may be anywhere from white to orange, and both sexes have long white whiskers. Males also sport a 3-inch (8 cm) white-tipped black crest on the top of the head, which becomes erect when it's time to make clear who's in charge.

These fur seals spend a lot of time on land. They choose storm-whipped rocky beaches beneath high cliffs for their breeding grounds. In September the males stake out their territories, and the rest of the herd shows up over the next two months. Pups are born between the end of November and February; the cows mate about a week after their pups are born and then go back to the sea. Adults molt after breeding, and by April most have left the breeding grounds.

South American fur seal bulls like this one (far left) select and defend territories along rocky shores. As a species, these are gentle, trusting animals, but in their occasional conflicts with Southern sea lions, with which they share their range, the fur seals generally win. Sea lions sometimes eat the fur seal pups and female South American fur seals are polygamous.

Fur seals generally prefer rocky coasts, as this Antarctic fur seal demonstrates. They prefer to pup in caves or under sheltering rocky overhangs where such are available.

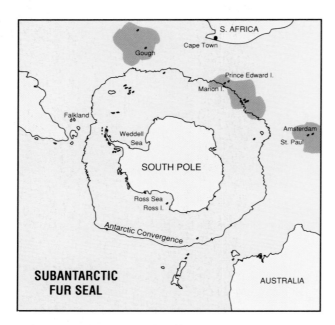

Pups are black with black whiskers at birth. They nurse until the next pup is born, approximately ten to eleven months later. Their mothers take good care of them, moving them into the shade when it's hot and defending them against all comers, at least for the first few weeks.

These fur seals eat squid, krill, fish, and rockhopper penguins. There are no known predators—though, as always, sharks and killer whales come under heavy suspicion.

Ninety-three percent of all subantarctic fur seals breed on Gough Island, about 1,400 miles (2,300 km) southeast of Capetown. A few also breed on Marion Island, and there is a possibility that they may interbreed with the antarctic fur seal, *A. gazella*. Harems have been reported with both species, and animals that are the size of antarctic fur seals with the unusual colors of the subantarctic fur seals have been photographed, though no specimens have been taken.

The worldwide population is 214,000 and growing nicely.

Antarctic Fur Seal

(Arctocephalus gazella)

The antarctic fur seal may be the biggest ecological recovery story in the world of pinnipeds, bigger even than the comeback of the northern elephant seal. Reported by Captain James Cook as "pretty numerous" in 1775, they were nearly extinct by the time the sealing industry finished with them in the 1820s, after 1,250,000 seals had been killed. Yet today, they number nearly 400,000, and the South Georgia rookery is probably the fastest growing seal colony on Earth.

Most antarctic fur seals are grayish-brown, easily our most popular color for seals, but a few individuals are pure white. These are not albinos, for the undercoat and skin are brown. Males are three times the size of females, 310 pounds (140 kg) versus 110 (50 kg).

Bulls arrive on South Georgia to homestead the breeding grounds. Waterfront properties are the choice parcels of real estate, as is true all over the world. Johnny-come-latelies, both literally and socially, find themselves with lots below the high tide line or off in the suburbs among the tussocks of grass. Like boys who douse themselves with cologne for the prom, the bulls give off a "pungent, musky, sweetish odor."

The cows arrive in early December, looking for space on a protected, pebbled beach. Insofar as a bull has secured a nice lot with waterfront access, he is likely to have a harem. Bulls don't gather cows—it would mean leaving their territory temporarily undefended—but they do try to keep any cows that happen by from leaving, a task that in-

Antarctic fur seals, like other fur seals, have a double coat of fur which, combined with a thick layer of blubber, provides excellent insulation against the cold.

The Antarctic fur seal colony on South Georgia Island is probably the most successful seal colony in the world, having gone from almost no seals in the 1820s to more than 400,000 today.

creases in difficulty in direct proportion to the number of cows that pass.

Most pups are born in December, within a day or so of the mother's arrival. They are born squeaking and hungry and set about looking for food without a lot of unnecessary dawdling. The pup has the mother to itself for a week. Then she mates and goes out to sea, returning every few days to nurse the pup. By mid-January, the rookery is virtually abandoned.

Bulls mature at four years but are not able to defend a desirable territory until they are eight or more. Cows bear their first pup at three or four.

One of the reasons that the antarctic fur seal is increasing so rapidly is the abundance of krill, their primary food. Researchers theorize that the decline of the baleen whale, which also eats krill, has made more krill than ever available for the fur seals. There's more food, hence more seals. They also eat

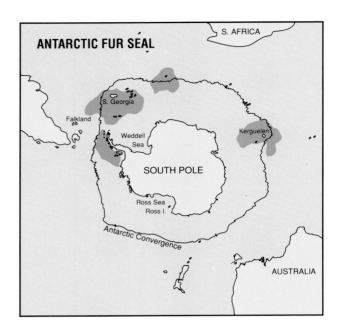

ANTARCTIC FUR SEAL

fish and squid. Now that they are no longer hunted, antarctic fur seals have no known predators, which also contributes significantly to their stunning return from the edge of extinction.

© Frank S. Todd/EarthViews

The Antarctic fur seal is usually found south of the Antarctic Convergence, that point where the cold water of the Antarctic sinks below the warmer water of the subantarctic. Once known as the Kerguelen fur seal because of large breeding grounds on Kerguelen Island, it was re-christened the Antarctic fur seal because Kerguelen Island is now the only island in its range on which it does *not* breed.

Cape Fur Seal/Australian Fur Seal

(Arctocephalus pusillus)

Arctocephalus pusillus is found both on the southernmost coasts of Africa around the Cape of Good Hope and along the coasts of New South Wales (Australia) and Tasmania. There are few distinguishing characteristics between the seals in each area—one, to be precise—but the populations are so far apart that they have achieved subspecies status on that ground alone. *A. p. pusillus* is the Cape fur seal of Africa, and *A. p. doriferus* is the Australian fur seal of New South Wales.

These are the largest of all the fur seals, the bulls a little short of 8 feet (2.3 m) long and nearly 800 pounds (350 kg) in weight, the females about a third that weight. They are dark gray above and paler below. The pups are born black.

There are some seals at the rookery all year, but many more arrive during the breeding season in early December. Cows nurse their pups for about a week before going to sea. The pups nurse until the next pup is born, sometimes as long as two years, though the pups begin foraging for themselves at five months. By seven months, they can spend two or three days at sea on their own.

The cows mate about a week after the pup is born but do not become pregnant until four months later. Females have their first pup at four, and males are also mature by four. Young bulls are not able to win their battles for territory until they are eight to twelve, so bulls in that awkward in-between stage—old enough to mate but unable to—hang around on the fringes of the rookery being rowdy and noisy, for all the world like a gang of kids revving motorcycles. They also play like kids, sliding on slippery rocks and chasing around on the beach.

These fur seals only eat between two and three weeks each month, and for the two months of the breeding season, the breeding bulls don't eat at all. They eat fish, squid, octopus, rock lobsters, and stones. Since the highest quantities of stones are found in the stomachs of yearlings, it has been suggested that they eat the rocks to ease their hunger pangs when their mothers are away at sea. Cape fur seals are surface feeders, rarely diving deeper than 150 feet (45 m); Australian fur seals dive much deeper, to at least 400 feet (120 m).

Australian fur seals do not migrate from the rocky shores of Tasmania, Victoria, and New South Wales. Although virtually identical to the South African or Cape fur seal, they are considered a separate species because the two populations are so far apart.

AUSTRALIAN FUR SEAL

Seals too young to breed only come ashore to molt in December and January, spending most of their first three years at sea dodging the great white sharks that are their primary predator. Killer whales also attack the Australian fur seal.

The Australian fur seal is fully protected and has been since 1881, after sealing had decimated the herds. The Cape fur seal is preyed upon by black-backed jackals, brown hyenas, and people. It is hunted under licenses issued by the government of South Africa, and the hunts take place both summer and winter. Quotas are established and licenses issued under the inappropriately named Sea Birds and Seal Protection Act of 1973. Two thousand bulls are taken each year, and 60 percent of the pups.

© Charles G. Summers/Gerry Ellis Wildlife Collection

For the most part, seals, including New Zealand fur seals (left and opposite page), do not drink water, either fresh or sea water. Even when catching fish or squid or crustaceans, they manage to swallow almost no water. Having stated the rule, there are exceptions. The New Zealand fur seals found in New Zealand do not drink sea water, but those on South Neptune Island, Australia, do.

New Zealand Fur Seal

(Arctocephalus forsteri)

The New Zealand fur seal was named for the botanist on Captain James Cook's second voyage, George Forster. Forster sketched the "sea bear" in 1773, but not until nearly a century later were specimens collected and the scientific description of a new species published. Such was the rapacity of the sealers that all the seals on Macquarie Island, discovered in 1810, were gone entirely by 1820. They did not breed there again until 1955, 135 years later. The New Zealand fur seal has been protected since 1875, and today the population is approaching 40,000.

These fur seals are gray-brown, but their white-tipped top-coat hairs give them a silvery sheen. The pups are born black. Bulls are more than twice the weight of cows and are a little over 6½ feet (2 m) long.

The young seals and cows stay at the rookeries most of the year, leaving for a few days at a time to feed. In spring (October), the breeding bulls arrive to strut and roar and do battle for their territories. The cows come to pup in December, and pups are born through the middle of January. Birth takes between six and ten minutes.

The pups are nursed for about ten days, before the mother goes to sea to feed for three or four days. The temporarily bereft pups gather in their own groups, and their mothers come to find them when they return from feeding. The pups nurse until the next pup is born the following year. The cows mate a week after the birth of their pups. By January, the breeding bulls have gone two and a half months without feeding, and they are finally hungry enough to head back out to sea, their duty to another generation done.

The New Zealand fur seal eats squid, octopus, lamprey eels, crab, rock lobster, and penguins. They do not eat much fish, and the exceptions are rarely of commercial value, which does not stop the local fishermen from accusing them bitterly. They have no known predators besides humans, and the only killing done today is for scientific research.

NEW ZEALAND FUR SEAL

NEW ZEALAND

Coromandel Peninsula

Wellington

Christchurch

Solander I.

Stewart I.

Macquarie I.

For eighteen years the Russian sealer Gerassim Pribilof searched the Bering Sea for the Mist Islands which an old Aleut *shaman* had told him were home to millions of fur seals. The Bering Sea is where the warm Gulf Stream meets the icy Arctic drift, and a thick fog rises like smoke from a prairie fire. For seventeen seasons Pribilof searched without success, until finally, in 1786, he found them by following the roaring sound of millions of bulls, a noise that could be heard five or six miles (8 or 9.5 km) out to sea. He took their lives and their hides, and gave them his name. The seal is often called the Pribilof fur seal, the islands are known as the Pribilof Islands.

© Gerry Ellis/Ellis Wildlife Collection

Northern Fur Seal

(Callorhinus ursinus)

For more than three centuries this has been the fur of the most luxurious sealskin coats. When discovered in 1786 by the Russian navigator Gerassim Pribilof, the northern fur seal numbered two and a half million. Both their major breeding grounds, the Pribilof Islands, and the fur seal he found there carry his name. *Callorhinus ursinus* has a collection of aliases, including Pribilof fur seal, northern fur seal, and Alaska fur seal.

Northern fur seals are dark brown if they're male, dark gray if they're female, and both have a light patch on the chest. Pups are born with a black coat, which is shed at two months for one that is pale gray on the back and creamy on the belly. Males acquire the dignity of a mane at the age of six.

Pups are born in June and July and stick very close to their mothers for the first week. After that, the cows go to sea six days a week, coming back once a week to nurse. Since suckling amounts to a rare treat, the pups take as much as a gallon (4.5 liters) at a time. Pup pods try to find a place in the rookery out of the way of the adults and spend most of their time sleeping or playing together. They can swim as soon as they're born but generally avoid the water until they are a month old.

Pups are born within two days of the cow's arrival in the rookery. They get about a week's worth of attention from their mothers, and none whatsoever from the bulls. Cows feed only their own pups, but how they determine which one is theirs in a pup pod of thousands of virtually identical pups has scientists baffled. The cow comes ashore where she left her pup the last time, gives a call that is the equivalent of "Dinner's on!" and every hungry pup for blocks around comes running. She seems to sort them out by sniffing each one's nose until she finds her own. Though the pups will cheerfully nurse from any mother that will let them, the mothers scoop the small imposters aside with no hesitation.

Harems develop more because the cows gather together than because of any efforts made by the bulls. The bulls bluff and bluster about, never leaving their territory undefended, going without food for two months. Younger bulls, whippersnappers and rakes with neither property nor position, hang around on the edges of the rookery hoping to waylay any female who gets close enough. Cows mate about a week after giving birth, but the blastocyst is not implanted for four months.

Females bear their first pup at five. Males mature at six, begin breeding at eight, but do not become harem masters before twelve, a position they may hold until they are twenty. Northern fur seals live thirty years and more.

They feed on the open sea, usually at night, sleeping during the day. They eat herring, squid, pollack, lantern fish, rock fish, cod, and lamprey eels. As is so often the case, salmon fishermen complain loud and long that they eat salmon, but food studies do not substantiate the accusations.

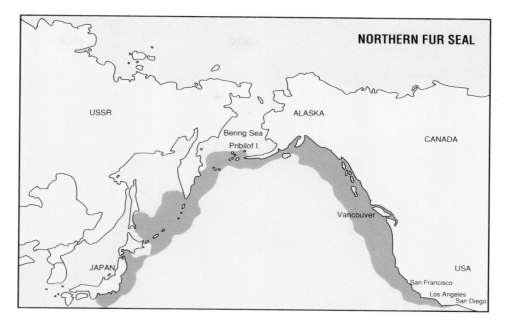

NORTHERN FUR SEAL

Both Soviet and American sealing devastated the northern fur seal, reducing a population of 2.5 million to 200,000. An agreement negotiated by the United States, the U.S.S.R., Japan, and Canada in 1911 prohibited taking the seals at sea. In 1957 the agreement was renegotiated, and today only the Soviet Union and the United States hunt the northern fur seal under limited quotas determined by the number of pups born each year. Canada and Japan each receive 15 percent of the kill. Today the total population is estimated at 1.8 million, another astonishing proof of the ability of other species to return from the brink of oblivion if only people will allow them to do so.

A wide open mouth displaying sharp teeth is a threat display, warning intruders away from this Northern fur seal's territory. Seals' teeth reflect their age and their health by laying down annual rings, very much like the rings found on trees. Experts can determine sex, age, health, sexual maturity, and pregnancy, as well as feeding and fasting patterns by examining the thickness of the dentine rings on a seal's teeth.

Chapter Four

Walruses

Given that there are some 4,000 species of mammals on Earth, it's no wonder that a few of them—the rhinoceros and the duckbilled platypus, for example—appear to have been designed more for function than for beauty. Perhaps, considering the survival value of function, it is more surprising that animals like panthers and peacocks exist at all. Aesthetic speculation aside, it is clear to the most untutored eye that the walrus was not designed for beauty. It is, plainly put, one of the homeliest creatures ever to grace this planet. Weighing a tad over a ton (2,673 lbs/1,215 kg), the walrus looks like nothing so much as an enormous leather bag with tusks and a mustache. By an astonishing and felicitous coincidence of language, the Eskimos call walruses' traditional hauling out sites *ugli*.

Walruses come in two flavors, *Odobenus rosmarus rosmarus,* found in the North Atlantic, and *Odobenus rosmarus divergens,* endemic to the North Pacific.

One writer called this walrus summer haul-out on Round Island, Alaska, the Bristol Bay Men's Club (far left). Members are male walrus only, no cows or pups allowed. It's understandable; at mid-molt the males are nearly naked, and not exactly at their most attractive.

© John W. Warden

The Latin name for the walrus, *Odobenus,* means *tooth walker*. It comes from the walrus' habit of using their tusks to haul themselves out of the water onto ice or to climb rocks on land. Walrus tusks are typically abraded where they have been dragged across the ocean floor as the walrus snuffle up the sand or gravel and feel for shellfish with their sensitive whiskers. Walrus tusks were once more valuable than elephant ivory, or even gold.

Walruses are exclusively creatures of the Arctic; none are found in the Antarctic. The two subspecies are distinguished largely by distribution, which is to say the Pacific walrus is never found in the Atlantic, and vice versa. The Pacific walrus is slightly bigger and has a wider skull and longer tusks.

The walrus has been known for more than 2,000 years; the Atlantic walrus holds the distinction of having been classified by Linnaeus himself in 1758. The Pacific walrus was not recognized as a separate subspecies until 1815.

Walruses once inhabited the coasts of northern Europe—William Caxton reported a walrus being taken in the Thames in 1456. The name *walrus* comes from the Scandinavian *hvalross,* meaning whale horse. Walrus hide, an inch thick and so tough musket balls bounced off it, was preferred for warriors' shields even over bronze. Sailing ships that plied the North Atlantic were rigged with ropes of walrus hide and their seams sealed with tar rendered from walrus fat. The tusks, found on all walruses, male and female alike, were used as currency in their natural form and intricately carved into *objets d'art* for more than twenty centuries. Their very usefulness caused walruses to be hunted until, today, they are no longer found on the European continent.

The North Atlantic walrus is found in the eastern Canadian Arctic at the north end of Hudson Bay and in Greenland in the Thule area. Some are also found on the west coast of Greenland and on the coast of Novaya Zemlya off the Soviet Union, but hunting decimated the walrus in these areas, and only a few thousand are believed to remain despite recent laws passed in Greenland to protect them. The Pacific walrus frequents the Bering and Chukchi seas, the arctic seas bordered by Alaska and the Soviet Union. Today the greatest concentration of walruses haul out on Wrangel Island in the East Siberian Sea. There is also a small population found in the Laptev Sea off the coast of Siberia, which has led to the suggestion that a third subspecies be recognized, *Rosmarus odobenus laptevi,* Chapskii, but the suggestion has not met with wide acceptance. The walrus of the Laptev is intermediate in size between the Pacific and Atlantic walruses. The total world population of walruses is estimated at 230,000, with 200,000 of these Pacific walruses, 25,000 Atlantic walruses, and perhaps 5,000 in the Laptev region.

Walruses spend very nearly their entire lives at sea, two thirds of it in arctic water. The other third is spent hauled out on drifting pack ice or on land, to rest, to give birth, and to molt. The Pacific walrus migrates

© John W. Warden

© John W. Warden

Walrus also use their tusks for fighting. The largest bulls with the biggest tusks frequently leave rivals with deep puncture wounds, despite their tough hide. They fight in water, like the two in the top photograph, for space to put on their mating display. They fight on land (below) to establish who's in charge. An odd fact: Males mostly dominate other males. Females are wooed with soft whistles and bell-like notes accompanying a walrus water ballet until they choose their mate.

from Bristol Bay off Alaska to Wrangel Island, a good 1,100 miles (1,800 km). Most of the distance is covered by swimming, but favorable winds and currents can move snow-covered ice floes northward in the spring, allowing the walruses to rest and cover many miles of the migration while taking their leisure. It sounds like an exotic and curious way to travel, but winds and currents being what they are—which is to say wayward, willful, and given to following their own whims—walruses hauled out on the ice to rest may well find themselves drifting south instead of north for days or even weeks at a time.

Walruses swim at approximately 6.2 miles per hour (10 km/h), so a walrus swimming industriously could presumably cover the distance in seven or eight days, if it swam without resting. However, they typically meander north feeding, swimming, and resting at a leisurely and dignified pace. They swim most determinedly when there are no con-

venient ice floes to rest on and during storms. On the southern migration, the ice is often too thin to support the weight of the walruses, so they swim ahead of the pack ice, making their way through open water. Atlantic walruses do not migrate so far as is known.

Walruses use their tusks rather like arms, to heave themselves out of the water onto the ice or to climb up rocky embankments. They do not use them to dig up food from the sea floor. In fact, their method of feeding is far more strange and curious: walruses stand on their heads underwater, using their whiskers to ferret out small shellfish like clams and cockles; they then suck the meat out of the shell. Walruses suck so hard that they create a vacuum of no less than one negative atmosphere. Think of foraging walruses as the vacuum cleaners of the sea. They consume between 110 and 187 pounds (50–85 kg) of food per day, and one knowledgeable researcher estimated that if all the walruses in the world were to feed simultaneously, they would consume a billion clams a day. They feed mostly in shallow coastal waters, rarely deeper than 240 feet (73 m), for eight to twelve hours a day. Occasionally, rogue walruses, usually males, eat young bearded or ring seals, narwhal, or even cannibalize young walruses, but it has not been clearly determined whether the meat they eat is carrion or the animals were killed by the walruses. These rogues are easy to spot because their tusks and skin are grease-stained by the fat of the seals.

Walruses also use their tusks to threaten and to fight, to drive an intruder from a choice resting place on the ice, or, by big males, to clear a path through the herd. Males fight over females, and mothers defend their babies, but except in the battles between adult males during mating season, most of the wounds are surface scratches, rather than serious tears or punctures. To a large extent, the very toughness of their hides keeps them from doing each other any significant harm. Until the passage of the Marine Mammal Act in 1972, walrus hide was used to make buffing wheels for silver and other metals. Its tough, thick, fibrous, and abrasive surface was better suited to the purpose than any of the synthetic materials that have replaced it. It was also used for machine belts, harnesses, boot leather, and the tips of billiard cues. A century ago, the finest carriage traces were made from walrus hide; a narrow strip cut in a spiral from a single hide made a rope an inch thick (2.5 cm), 100 yards long (91 m), and virtually unbreakable. Anthropologist F. G. Rainey described this rope as "the strongest line known before the invention of the steel cable."

Walrus courtship is a noisy affair. Females gather in small groups on the ice floes, and the males pick a place in the water just off the floe to give their display. This ritual has a number of the elements of courtship in Latin countries, where the young women gather demurely in a public promenade, and the young men swagger and strut to display their charms. Just as the young men will talk loudly and engage in wolf whistles and other signs of male approbation, so the walruses make growling and barking sounds at the surface and a soft whistle before submerging to perform the dance of desire in a walrus water ballet. Each display occupies the space of some two or three minutes and includes underwater clicks, rasps, and knocks, accompanied by bell-like notes, a veritable walrus serenade. Males come equipped with their own sound equipment, pharyngeal pouches in the cheeks that resonate and amplify sound, the walrus equiva-lent of turning up the volume on a boom box. (The pharyngeal pouches occur only in male walruses; no other pinniped is known to have them.) If one male enters another's territory, a fierce battle ensues, with great grunts and roars and splashing and slashing of tusks until one or the other beats a re-treat. If a female is sufficiently charmed by a suitor's song and dance, she slips into the water with him. Mating takes place in the chill water of the arctic seas between Janu-ary and March.

As with other pinnipeds, a blastocyst is formed but implantation of the fetus is de-layed about four months. Pregnancy, from fertilization to birth, is at least fifteen to six-teen months long, an unusually lengthy pe-riod for mammals, and possibly unique among pinnipeds. (Only the Australian sea lion, *Neophoca cinerea*, may have a preg-nancy of similar duration.)

Most walruses are born between mid-April and mid-June. Pacific walrus babies are born smack in the middle of the spring mi-gration on a southbound ice floe. Tempera-tures average between 32° and 41° F. (0°–5° C.), and the water is 29° F. (–1.5° C.).

Walrus are thigmo-tactic, a big word that means they love touch-ing. Even when there's plenty of room, they prefer to lay in humongous heaps, one on top of the other, piled every which way, their tusks propped on their nearest neighbor. The middle of the pile is consid-ered the choicest piece of real estate, and dominant bulls do not hesitate to bulldoze their 3,000 pounds (1,350 kg) over anyone in the way.

© John W. Warden

Walrus have the longest pregnancy of any pinniped—fifteen months—and they care for their infants longer than any other seal—two years or more. The mothers defend their babies fiercely, refusing to abandon them even in the face of mortal danger. Females use their tusks to herd their babies along in front of them and to fight against predators like polar bears and killer whales. Even the babies have tusks. The tusks continue to grow throughout the walrus' lives and can eventually reach more than three feet (1 m) long and as thick as a man's wrist.

The weather is usually fair and sunny. Newborn walruses weigh in at a hefty 140 pounds (63 kg) and are 4 feet (1.2 m) long, not exactly petite. By comparison, newborn elephant seals, the largest pinniped, are the same length at birth but weigh a maximum of 99 pounds (45 kg).

The bond between mother and calf is stronger among walruses than any other pinniped—perhaps any other mammal, with the possible exception of elephants and people. The mother nurses her baby for two to three years before it becomes independent. (Compare this with the hooded seal, which nurses its young for four days!) Walrus milk is not as rich as that of other marine mammals, being about one-third fat, but even so, the calves gain about 35 pounds (16 kg) a month on milk alone. Walrus mothers take good care of their little ones, defending them fiercely, herding them away from danger, and even adopting orphaned pups. Reports of stupendous courage come from even the most carefully objective scientific reports. Francis H. Fay, the leading American researcher on the Pacific walrus, tells of accompanying Eskimos on a walrus hunt. "In some 50 encounters between Eskimos and walrus cows with young calves, I observed only six separations that resulted in

the calves being captured while the mothers escaped, apparently unharmed. On one occasion, a small herd was stampeded into the water, leaving behind an injured calf imprisoned in a smooth-sided crater in the ice. After a few minutes, one of the cows returned to the floe, emerged from the water, and approached the barking calf, even to within 2 m (6.5 ft) of the waiting hunters. This cow was shot . . ."

When threatened by predators, whether hunters or polar bears, cows often herd and push the calves into the water before entering themselves. J. J. Burns reported in 1965, "The hollering of the calves can be heard at a considerable distance, and the older animals continue to return to the edge of the ice until the last of the noisy calves has been encouraged to leave." When calves bark frantically, walruses come from all around to find out what's the matter, and orphaned calves are sometimes rescued by other walruses, including males, who tuck them under their chests with their foreflippers and carry them off to safety.

The only other predator of the walrus is the killer whale. Walrus mothers carry their calves on their backs while swimming, and Charles H. Scammon, the famous nineteenth-century whaling captain, reported in 1874

© John W. Warden

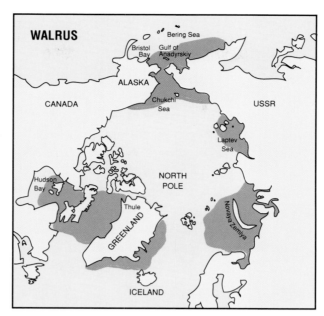

In 1603 a sailor named Jonas Poole sailing for the English Muscovy Company recorded finding walrus hauled out on Bear Island, 300 miles (480 km) north of Norway: ''We saw a sandy bay in which we came to anchor. We had not furled our sails but we saw many morses [walrus] swimming by our ship and heard withal so huge a noise of roaring as if there had been a hundred lions. It seemed very strange to see such a multitude of monsters of the sea lie like hogs in heaps . . .'' That description, written some four hundred years ago, would stand to describe these walrus at Round Island, Alaska.

seeing killer whales dislodge the calf from the mother's back by ramming her from below. Killer whales attack in the water as wolves do on land, by surrounding and separating small groups or individuals from the herd and attacking as a group. Some of the whales grab the walrus's flippers in their teeth while others ram the walrus from below with their heads. It is, in effect, a marine mugging. Walruses have been found alive with every bone in their bodies broken by killer whales, though most die when their ribs are smashed and the broken ribs puncture their lungs. To fully appreciate the magnitude of the ramming power required to accomplish this, it's important to know that Eskimos hunting walruses use full-metal-jacketed bullets to penetrate the tough hide and dense bone of the walrus.

Walruses do not take killer whale attacks lying down. Lacking Guardian Angels corps to make the seas safe for walruses, they fight back with their tusks. Another whaling captain observed a pair of killer whales attacking an adult female walrus with three young. The pups ''were crawling on the back of the adult, which kept turning its head toward the *orcae*, threatening them with its tusks.'' The moral of the story is, don't mess around with a walrus mom.

Obviously, being born onto ice well north of the Arctic Circle makes keeping warm a high priority. Walruses have no fur to speak of, so the mother warms the infant with her body, clasping it to her breast between her foreflippers. Walruses are insulated from the cold largely by a layer of blubber nearly 3 inches (6–7 cm) thick and by a circulatory system that can heat the core while keeping the skin surface just warm enough to prevent damage. There can be as much as

75° F. (24° C.) difference between the temperature of the skin and the internal temperature of the animal.

Largely due to their ability to regulate the amount of blood that reaches the surface, walruses have the magical ability to change color. Their basic color is cinnamon brown, but by withdrawing the blood from the skin to maintain core body temperature, they can turn a ghostly white, making themselves appear to be albino. (Albinos have white skin or fur and pink eyes, and the permanently bloodshot eyes of the walrus makes this seem a perfectly reasonable, though completely wrong, assumption.) By bringing the blood to the surface to release excess heat, they turn themselves a bright pink. (This often leads observers to the erroneous conclusion that they are sunburned.) Isn't it lovely to live in a world that offers such delicious curiosities as pink and white walruses?

When hauled out, a walrus herd resembles nothing so much as the world's largest football pileup. They lie next to, underneath, and on top of each other in great heaps, even when there is plenty of room on the ice or beach. In general, they clump in three separate groups: adult males, adolescent males, and females, with the young of both sexes herding with the females.

The first mention of the walrus in Western literature is found in the *Speculum Regale*, published in the thirteenth century, in which they are identified as related to seals. About the middle of the eighteenth century, scientists questioned classifying the walrus with the pinnipeds and advanced theories linking them, variously, with whales, sea cows, and even the platypus. It wasn't until the nineteenth century that they were safely ensconced once again among the pinnipeds. The first drawing of a walrus to appear in Europe was done by the famed artist Albrecht Dürer, who probably used as his model the pickled walrus head sent as a present by the Bishop of Trondheim to Pope Leo X in 1520. The first live walrus was exhibited at the London Zoo in 1853, but it only lived a few days.

Since then, zoo-keeping practices have improved enormously, and walruses are such charming, friendly, and curious animals that they invariably become great favorites of their keepers.

Walrus live nearly their entire lives at sea, about two-thirds of it in the water. While most Pacific walrus migrate as far north into the Chukchi Sea as the ice allows, 15,000 bulls haul out at a traditional *ugli* on Round Island in the Bering Sea thirty-three miles (53 km) off the coast of Alaska. There they molt and eat, for these waters are their summer feeding grounds. Walrus consume between 110 and 187 pounds (50 and 85 kg) of shellfish per day. These fascinating animals have been called by many names: morse, russmorsi, sea tusker, Beast of the Great Teeth, sea cow, *vache marin*, and *hvalross*, Scandinavian for whale-horse, whence comes our walrus.

Visiting the Walrus in the Wild

To see bull walruses hauled out, head for
Round Island in Alaska's Walrus Islands
State Game Sanctuary. It's 400 miles (644
km) southwest of Anchorage in Bristol Bay
at the edge of the Bering Sea. You'll need a
visitor's permit from the Alaska Department
of Fish and Game (Box 1030, Dillingham,
Alaska 99576), a warm sleeping bag, and a
good quality waterproof, rip-stop nylon tent
with extra-long stakes, capable of with-
standing 75-mile-per-hour winds. This is a
wilderness adventure; there are no facilities
and no phones. Just two park rangers, a
world of arctic wildflowers, a quarter-million
nesting birds—including bald eagles, puffins
and auklets—red foxes, Steller's sea lions,
and 15,000 bull walruses. Call Alaska Air-
lines (1-800-426-0333) and tell them you
need to get to Togiak Cannery by way of Dillingham, and they'll know how to get you
there. Call Don Winkleman, of Don's Round
Island Boat Charters, to get the last 33 miles
(53 km) from Togiak Cannery to Round Island (in summer, 907-493-5127; in winter,
907-596-3420).

Chapter Five

Elephant Seals

The elephant seal is the sort of creature one expects to find in the pages of a medieval bestiary sooner than on the beaches of California. Its looks are nothing less than bizarre. It is, if you will, the giraffe of marine mammals, except that for all their oddity, giraffes at least have a certain grace and sweetness of temperament. Viewed from a distance elephant seals can scarcely be distinguished from coastal rocks. In the ocean they bear a disconcerting resemblance to the sea monsters that ancient cartographers drew to lend a little color to their depictions of the *terra incognita* of the New World. Found in large numbers at the Ano Nuevo Reserve in California, the elephant seal is relatively easy to observe in the wild.

Elephant seals invite superlatives. They are the largest of all the seals, with adult males weighing as much as 6,000 pounds (2,727 kg) and stretching to a length of 15 feet (4.6 m). There is an unverified report of an elephant seal bull

This is a classic instance of "push come to shove" (far left). Northern elephant seals are not aggressive with people—I have seen students from the University of California at Santa Cruz working among them and the seals scarcely bothered to lift their heads. But male-to-male is another story. The first Northern elephant seal battle I saw, one male bloodied the other, drove him into the sea, and then patrolled the shore for half an hour to make sure he didn't come back.

Weaned pups like these two (above) gather in groups called "weaner pods" for two or three months after their mothers leave. During that time, they go without food entirely until they learn to fish for themselves. They fast unwillingly, often trying to sneak a meal from a mother who is still nursing, but they generally get cuffed, nipped, and chased off. This youngster appears to be filing a protest at the general unfairness of things.

22 feet (6.8 m) long. The females, petite by comparison, weigh 1,700 pounds (773 kg), not even a third the weight of the males, and are 11 feet (3.4 m) long.

They also dive deeper than any other seal species has been known to go. One female was monitored to 4,200 feet (1,292 m), more than three-quarters of a mile (1.3 km) down, before the recording device failed. The previous diving record was held by Antarctica's Weddell seal at 1,950 feet (600 m), less than half as far as the elephant seal went.

Researchers, curious to know how deep seals could dive and how long they could stay down, tried using captive seals in laboratory experiments to find out. Unfortunately, what they observed turned out to reveal more about the effects of terror on laboratory seals than how seals process oxygen and carbon dioxide to dive to great depths and stay down for long periods of time. Dr. Kit Kovacs, University of Waterloo, Canada, explains, "Much of the early research on diving in pinnipeds was conducted on restrained animals in the laboratory. Very recent research on less stressed, freely diving seals suggests that much of the early research on forced dives was not entirely applicable to animals in nature. Many of the

observations arose because the animals were restrained and frightened and had no control over the duration of their dives." Not only were the laboratory seals terrified, but the data obtained has been proved virtually worthless. The difficulty arises from the fact that time/depth recorders are expensive pieces of equipment, which compels scientists to restrict their studies on wild animals to those species reliable enough to come back to the same place they left from, and accessible enough that the recorders can be attached to the seal and recovered. Elephant seals fit these parameters nicely, and the research on diving conducted by Dr. Burney LeBoeuf at the University of California, Santa Cruz, has illuminated the facts of northern elephant seals' ability to dive to astonishing depths far beyond anything previously known or even surmised.

Northern elephant seals also fast longer than almost any other seal, as much as four months of the year. The males fast for three months during the breeding season, losing about one third of their body weight; that is, one ton (0.9 metric tons). They fast again during the month-long molting period. Mother seals fast for a month during the breeding season. During that period, between

fasting and feeding her pup, the mother loses 330 to 440 pounds (150–200 kg). For every pound the mother loses, her pup gains two. The busily nursing pup quadruples its birth weight in less than a month, drinking approximately 287 pounds (130 kg) of milk and retaining 230 pounds (100 kg) of that as blubber. Once weaned, the pup fasts for two to three months, living entirely off its blubber. Females and weaners, as the weaned pups are called, also fast during the molt.

The elephant seals of Ano Nuevo are one of the great comeback stories of ecological history, going from as few as twenty in the 1890s to over 100,000 today.

Commercial hunting of the northern elephant seal began in 1818 on Guadalupe Island off the Pacific coast of Baja California; by 1860 there were too few left for the sealers to bother with. The elephant seals were second choice as far as the sealers were concerned. The real lure of Guadalupe Island between 1800 and 1820 had been the Guadalupe fur seal, but in those twenty years the bulk of the fur seal population was exterminated.

In 1818 the sealers began supplementing the declining fur seal catch with the elephant seal, rendering its blubber for oil. The oil was used to light parlor and street lamps, to lubricate machinery, to tan leather, and to manufacture clothing, soap, and paint. It was considered second only to the prized oil of sperm whales. A single bull might render 210 gallons (80 dl) of oil. By 1860, contemporary writers reported the northern elephant seal nearly extinct.

A small herd of 419 elephant seals on Cedros Island off the west coast of Baja California was wiped out in 1880, the last few being taken as scientific specimens. Those specimens clearly established the northern

The northern elephant seal breeding grounds at Ano Nuevo Island off the coast of California (left) were recolonized in 1961 with the birth of two pups. The island rookery is now filled to capacity, and in 1975, the first pups were born on mainland beaches across from the island. Those beaches have been declared a state reserve, and guided tours take visitors to within twenty feet (6m) of these strange and wonderful creatures. The first time I went to Ano Nuevo I saw a cow give birth and watched the sea gulls quarrel over the afterbirth. I also watched two bulls roar and fight until one finally drove the other into the sea.

elephant seal as a separate and distinct species from the southern elephant seal of South Georgia Island and Kerguelen Island in the Antarctic.

In May 1892, Dr. Charles H. Townsend of the American Museum of Natural History in New York, engaged in a fur seal collecting expedition, found and killed specimens of the Guadalupe fur seal. He brought back four skulls, which were identified five years later as a new species and named after him, *Arctocephalus townsendi*. It was 1928 before any member of the scientific community saw another living Guadalupe fur seal or, indeed, had a clue as to what the animal looked like.

On the same expedition, Dr. Townsend found what he had reason to believe were the last eight northern elephant seals alive. The expedition killed seven of the eight on the grounds that there were very few specimens in museums and the species was doomed anyway. Since it had already been

identified as a species in 1866 and named *Mirounga angustirostris,* it could not be named after Dr. Townsend.

Fortunately, Dr. Townsend was wrong in his conviction that the species was doomed. He returned to Guadalupe Island in May 1911 to find a remnant breeding population of 125 northern elephant seals. That same year the Mexican government, in an act of remarkable ecological farsightedness, extended the seals partial protection and in 1922 granted them full protection.

Scientists believe that the total population of northern elephant seals in 1890 may have been as few as twenty animals and certainly no more than one hundred. From this tiny nucleus has come the current population of more than 100,000. When the seals began repopulating their traditional breeding grounds, extending their range to southern California, the United States also granted the northern elephant seal full protection. Today the Marine Mammal Protection Act

Mating among elephant seals is largely a matter of survival of the fattest. The biggest bulls drive off all smaller bulls and then take every opportunity to mate with every female they can lay flippers on. Females have few options in the matter. The males outweigh them three to one.

© Frank S. Balthis/Nature's Design

© Frank S. Balthis/Nature's Design

(1972) protects the seals in American waters, while Mexican law forbids any hunting or harassment of the seals in Mexican waters.

Ano Nuevo Island lies a half-mile off the northern California coast across a treacherous, rocky channel. It consists of 12 acres of Miocene cherty shale, rock that dates from approximately the same time that the first pinniped ancestors slipped back into the water, give or take a couple of million years. The island is approximately 842 feet (259 m) wide, a mere 36 feet (11 m) wide at its narrowest point. It is 1,287 feet (396 m) long, less than a quarter of a mile.

Tiny as it is, Ano Nuevo Island is the most important seal rookery and migratory resting place for hundreds of miles in either direction, north or south. It is used year-round by four species of seals: Steller's sea lions, California sea lions, harbor seals, and northern elephant seals. All but the California sea lions breed on the island.

Elephant seals began recolonizing Ano Nuevo Island in 1955, and the first two pups were born in 1961. In 1975, the first pup was born on the mainland. Today, hundreds upon hundreds of elephant seals are born and bred on the sandy beaches of Ano Nuevo Island as well as the mainland beaches of Ano Nuevo State Reserve.

Elephant seal bulls begin arriving for the breeding season in early December, the females in mid-December. The pregnant females usually give birth to a single pup within six days of arrival. Mothers nurse their pups daily for approximately a month. They come into estrus for four days during the last week of nursing. On the last day of estrus, thirty-four days after her arrival, the mother weans her pup by going back out to sea. The pups, which have grown so fat they can scarcely move, gather together and try to stay out of the way of the battling bulls.

Elephant seals are polygynous, with the dominant male overseeing a harem of as many as fifty females. These are not harems in the true sense of the word, for the bull has little control over the females. If they decide to move, he merely follows along.

Males establish their pecking order in December when they first arrive. They spend the rest of the three-month breeding season alternately doing battle to defend their social position, mating briefly, and sleeping. The lower-ranking males hang around on the periphery of the harems hoping to catch a departing female before she heads out to sea.

Dominance appears to be established on the basis of size—not simply of the animal's body, but of the curiously shaped appendage that gives the elephant seal its common name. This peculiar dangling appendage, suspended squarely over the seal's mouth, functions as a resonator for the bull's bellows, which sound distinctly like a motorcycle with a bad muffler. The sound carries for half a mile (1 km) and more and generally heralds a territorial battle. Battles are characterized by two bulls facing off and galumphing toward each other at full tilt. Having plowed into each other, the rivals endeavor to flip their foot-long noses out of the way and slash each other's necks and chests with their teeth. Occasionally, they bite their own noses in the process. Because the neck and chest are covered with a thick layer of blubber and a chest shield of callused, hardened skin, these encounters are sometimes bloody but rarely cause any serious harm to either combatant.

Because of the multiple matings, virtually all females are impregnated. The blastocyst is held in suspension for four months before implanting in the cow's uterus to begin the eight-month gestation.

Elephant seal cows do not eat from the time they arrive at the breeding grounds until they leave more than a month later. Pups weigh about 100 pounds (45 kg) at birth, and about 500 pounds (225 kg) at weaning, all of which comes from the mother's milk. The milk of the northern elephant seal is 54.4 percent fat. The pups nurse four to eight times a day.

By huddling together in a far corner, weaners reduce their chances of being crushed by a bull thundering heedlessly through the rookery. Over the next three months, they learn to swim and fend for themselves, and their departure in April and May coincides with a coastal upwelling when the sea is rich in food.

Elephant seals feed mainly at night on squid, small sharks, rays, and other deep water species. Because the Ano Nuevo breeding colony has been studied intensively since its inception, some very interesting observations have been made, one of which is that the presence of the seals appears to have increased the richness of the fishing grounds. The water just off Ano Nuevo is well known for both the size and the numbers of fish, and sport fishing boats in the area make a practice of fishing there. It is one more piece of documented evidence that, far from damaging fishing, as fishermen are apt to believe, seals actually increase the numbers of fish available.

Much of the research done on the elephant seals demonstrates Darwin's theory of survival of the fittest—in elephant seals that may be translated as survival of the fattest. The largest bulls win dominance battles and therefore mate with the largest number of females. (In the words of psychologist Frank Beach, "Coito, ergo sum.") It allows the largest females to win the safest places to bear and raise their pups, and the fattest pups have the best chance of living until they become competent swimmers and hunters.

The seals return to the sea in March and haul out again in May to molt. The molting is not a pretty process. Elephant seals have no fur, only skin, and the skin sloughs off in smelly, leprous patches. There is an awful story that circulates in seal circles about the nice people who, seeing a molting elephant

seal, decided it had some dread disease and shot it to put it out of its misery. The old skin is brown, the new pelage a handsome silver-gray. Once the seal is fully molted, it slips back out to sea, where it may wander as far north as Alaska and as far south as Mexico, but come December it will return to Ano Nuevo to begin the cycle of life.

Northern elephant seals have steadily expanded their range farther and farther north along the Pacific coast as their numbers have increased. Today their range extends from Isla Natividad in Baja California to Prince of Wales Island off Alaska. Breeding colonies exist from Isla Natividad north along the West Coast to the Farallon Islands off the northern California coast. There are elephant seal rookeries on the Channel Islands off Santa Barbara, at Ano Nuevo Island, Ano Nuevo State Reserve, Big Sur, the southeast Farallon Islands off the coast at San Francisco, and on mainland beaches at Point Reyes as well. Both Ano Nuevo Island and the Farallons are nature reserves with access restricted to researchers, but the elephant seals may be seen by the public at Ano Nuevo State Reserve where guided tours are offered. (Make reservations for tours at 415-879-0582.)

The recovery of the northern elephant seal is a gratifying example of the astonishing resilience of nature, and the amazing ability of a creature to survive against all odds, given nothing more than human acknowledgment—and enforcement—of its right to exist on the planet.

Visiting Elephant Seals

Oceanic Society Expeditions in San Francisco also takes tourists out to the Farallon Islands from July through September to see northern elephant seals, harbor seals, Steller's sea lions, and the occasional northern fur seal (and incidentally, whales, dolphins, tufted puffins, rhinoceros auklets, and a world of other living wonders). Northern elephant seals can also be seen at the opposite end of their range at Guadalupe and San Benito islands off Baja California. (Book through Oceanic Society Expeditions, 415-474-3385 for the Farallons, 415-441-1106 for Guadalupe and San Benito islands.)

Chapter Six

Harp Seal Watching at the Magdalen Islands

The ice below the helicopter looks as though it's been littered with scattered sausages. As the chopper lands we can see the chubby white harp seal pups that have looked at us so often and so appealingly from wildlife conservation posters. The harp seal whitecoat, with its winsome innocence and huge, dark eyes, is the world's leading symbol of the twentieth century's best effort at peaceful coexistence with the other living creatures of this planet. The unspeakable horror of men clubbing trusting, helpless babies to death is ended. In its place, tourists now participate in what is undoubtedly one of the world's premier wildlife experiences: walking unrestricted among the harp seals in their breeding grounds on the pack ice of Les Iles-de-la-Madeleine (the Magdalen Islands) of Canada.

When I visited this windswept, wintery nursery I was surprised at the quantity of small lumpish creatures with immense dark eyes lying about like so

For many years scientists were mystified as to how four-month-old harp seal pups (far left), migrating alone, can find their way 1,500 miles (2,400 km) north to summer feeding grounds they'd never seen. One possibility is that they follow schools of migrating fish, literally eating their way home. Because the pups make their way from ice floe to ice floe, hauling out to rest, it may be they simply follow the retreating ice north.

Harp seal pups, called "whitecoats" for obvious reasons, only retain their white fur for about two weeks. They become fat, like the appealing creature above, when they are about a week old. Once they begin to shed their pretty fur they are called "ragged jackets," for the old coat hangs on in patches and tufts and looks as patched and pieced as a beggar's coat. Once the spotted grey juvenile coat grows in they are called "greycoats."

many beguiling toys. The mother seals, silver-coated with the dark Irish harp marking on the back, are no match for their appealing offspring in the tourists' eyes. Everyone searches for a little one whose mother has gone for a quick swim in hopes of stroking it once or twice before its mother returns. The whitecoats wriggle away from the unfamiliar touch, yelping and turning and snapping like puppies acting tough. Their tiny teeth are no match for the thick gloves and boots required by temperatures that on a sunny day are around − 4° F. (− 20° C.), which, of course, does not include the wind chill factor.

Harp seals (*Phoca groenlandicus*) are seals of the Arctic ice, living between the sea and the drifting pack ice without ever touching land. The Latin name they were given in 1777 when they were first classified scientifically was *Pagophilus*, which means *ice lover*. Yet the harps spend only six weeks of the year—when they are whelping, mating, or molting—on the ice. For ten months of the year, they swim the northern seas. In one of the longest animal migrations we

know of, harp seals swim more than 3,000 miles (5,000 km) from the Canadian Arctic and the west coast of Greenland south to their whelping grounds on the ice off Les Iles-de-la-Madeleine in the Gulf of St. Lawrence. The new pups, once weaned and molted, make their way north to the summer feeding grounds independent of the adult seals. How they find their way is one of nature's most baffling mysteries. No one knows the answer, but the best guess so far is that they swim from ice floe to ice floe, following the ice north.

Harp seals give birth during the first three weeks of March on the pack ice that drifts south through the Gulf of St. Lawrence between Prince Edward Island and Newfoundland. Birth itself takes only seconds, typically lasting less than a minute. The pup is thrust unceremoniously from a cosy womb at a comfortable 98.6° F. (37° C.), out into temperatures that are often well below freezing. Because they are born with no layer of blubber to insulate them from the cold, the pups warm themselves first by shivering and then by burning what scien-

© Steven Morello

tists call ''brown fat'' to release internal heat without shivering. Brown fat produces heat by burning oxygen much faster than normal fat. Many hibernating animals use it to warm themselves when coming out of their dens after sleeping away the winter.

The pups conserve warmth and energy by doing what most newborns do: they sleep a lot, waking only to feed. The cry of a hungry pup is disconcertingly similar to the cry of a hungry baby. The pups nurse for about ten minutes every few hours. Mother seals seem to identify their pups by smell, nuzzling the pup's face with their noses immediately after birth and before each nursing. They nurse only their own pups, and a pup that is orphaned or abandoned is left to starve.

Harp seal milk is extremely rich. It looks a lot like plain yogurt, is very oily, and tastes like raw fish. It can be as much as 53 percent fat. Human milk, by comparison, is 3.5 percent fat, cow milk 3.4 percent. Marine mammals generally have high-fat milk, but even the blue whale's milk is only 38 percent fat.

Harp seal pups are born with no blubber and weigh 44 pounds (20 kg) at birth. They begin suckling within a few hours of being born and gain about 4½ pounds (2 kg) per day. By the time they are weaned, the pups weigh 75 pounds (34 kg) and have a blubber layer 2 inches (5 cm) thick.

The pups nurse for only twelve days before they are abruptly weaned. Weaning, in fact, is rather a misnomer, suggesting as it does a process of slow withdrawal. What actually happens is that the mothers simply disappear after two weeks, leaving the pups to learn to swim, forage, and travel 1,500 miles north to the summer feeding grounds on their own. The pups accept this only under serious protest: weaned pups cry, squawk, attempt to nurse from other mothers (getting themselves rudely cuffed in the process), huddle with other weaned pups, and generally make it clear to those in the vicinity that they've been wronged.

Forced to begin feeding, the pups hunt for tiny shrimp, sucking them into their mouths one at a time. While pups migrate all alone, older seals group together in pods to feed, eating both the tiny shrimp and fish such as

In the spring of 1844 Newfoundland sealers found a harp seal rookery off the southeast coast of Labrador that was no less than fifty miles (80 km) long and twenty miles (32 km) wide; a conservative estimate placed the number of seals there at more than 5,000,000. They were, of course, all females (like the one above) and pups, since the males remain in the water. Today, the total world population of harp seals is estimated at 2,500,000, less than half of what was found 150 years ago at a single welping patch.

capelin, herring, redfish, and polar cod. Capelin is fished commercially in such numbers that it may threaten the harp seals' food supply.

The whole process of birth, nursing, and mating takes only two weeks, an astonishingly brief period when compared with other animals. Cats and dogs, for example, take six weeks.

© Steven Morello

Back at the harp seal rookery, . . . dark leads of open water cleave the thick, glittering ice where the floes have broken or separated. A few mother seals bob to the surface to check on their pups, treading water as shining icicles form on their whiskers. Where leads have not formed, the mother seals chew through as much as 6 feet (1.8 m) of ice to create breathing holes. They are seldom out of earshot of their pups. When threatened, a mother seal rears up, opens her mouth to display a carnivore's teeth, and utters a low, guttural warning. If people keep walking toward them, they ordinarily slide into the water, but always stay close enough to keep an eye on their little ones.

On rare occasions a mother seal will charge, gripping the ice with her formidable claws and sliding swiftly across the ice. When our guide tried to drive a mother seal away from her pup, she gave a warning and then lunged. As he backed off, he stumbled on the ice, and she clipped him a good one on the knee, her teeth tearing through his survival suit and jeans to break the skin slightly. His pride more injured than his leg, the guide mumbled that in fifteen years of seal hunting, he'd never seen a harp seal attack to defend her pup. It rather served him right, since there were dozens of unattended pups, friendly and curious, who cheerfully mistook tourists for their mothers—the pup's definition of Mom seems to be *bigger than me*—and happily wriggled over for a closer look.

In most cases, a wide awake pup is a hungry pup, and they will cry for their mothers in what one scientist described as ''a remarkably human 'mmooooooomm' fashion.'' Harp seal milk looks like yogurt and tastes like fish. It is 40 percent fat, and the pups gain more than 4 pounds (2 kg) per day. On sunny days, the pups generate enough body heat to melt the snow beneath them. The melted snow then freezes into a pup-shaped cradle of ice.

These soulful eyes have done more to increase ecological awareness than anything since Rachel Carson's *Silent Spring*. Brian Davies, founder of the International Fund for Animal Welfare, saw his first seal hunt in 1964. Shocked and sickened by its barbaric savagery, he vowed to fight until the seal hunt was banned. It took more than 20 years of work before the European Economic Community (EEC) banned the importation of whitecoat pelts and ended the hunt by destroying the market for the skins. Wildlife posters featuring harp seal pups like this one helped turn the tide of public opinion against the harp seal hunt.

© Steven Morello

Some of the pups slept peacefully in ice cradles, smooth crystalline hollows sculpted by the body heat of the pudgy forms that occupied them. They slept in spite of a cacophony of sound: the wind whistling, the ice creaking and groaning, the territorial warnings of the mother seals, and the piteous mewling of wide-awake pups for more milk, more warmth, more Mom.

The transparent, hollow white hairs of a pup's fur function as a solar heater. The hairs transmit sunlight by reflecting it down to the pup's dark skin, which absorbs and retains the warmth. This solar radiation is remarkably effective: skin temperatures of 106° F. (41° C.) have been recorded in pups lying on the ice, in spite of the fact that a pup's normal body temperature is only 98.6° F. (37° C.) and the air temperature is often freezing. By using sunlight to keep warm, the pup saves energy by reducing the amount of calories that must be burned to maintain body warmth.

It is essential that a pup conserve absolutely every calorie it possibly can, because that's what goes into building the layer of blubber that insulates the pup to keep it warm. More importantly, the blubber is the pup's sole source of warmth and food between the time the mother seal leaves and the time the pup learns to forage and fend for itself, a period of two or three months of fasting.

This period of fasting coincides with the molt, which begins when the pup is three or four weeks old. During molting, seals replace both their fur and the surface layers of skin. All reports concur that the annual molt is a nasty process, itchy, foul-smelling, and mangy-looking. Harp seals gather in huge numbers in April and May to molt in three separate groups—males, young seals of both sexes, and females.

The pup's white coat falls out in tufts as the black-spotted silver coat begins to grow in. During the intermediate period, when they are neither pure white nor spotted silver, they are called ''ragged jackets.'' Once the new coat is grown in, they are called ''beaters.'' One researcher says that the name ''beater'' comes from the flailing and thrashing about the pups do in the process of learning to swim as they embark on the precarious process of fending for themselves. It is truly precarious; 20 to 30 percent of the pups do not live to see their first birthday. And those percentages, of course, are for natural mortality; they assume no hunting. Polar bears, Greenland sharks, and killer whales are a constant threat to pups and adult seals alike. If a pup survives its first year, it has a 90 percent chance of living out its full lifespan of thirty to thirty-five years.

The beaters molt again the following spring, when they are fourteen months old. The coat looks very much the same, but the molted pups are then referred to as ''bedlamers,'' a corruption of the French *bête de la mer*, which means ''sea beast.'' They keep the bedlamer pattern through three or four molts until they reach maturity at four or five years old. At that point the spots begin to fade and the distinctive black harp on their backs becomes readily recognizable. The harp marking appears quite suddenly in the males, but females often retain their spots for several years before the harp marking is distinct and clear. During the transition period from spots to harp, they are called ''spotted harps.''

Female harp seals usually bear their first pup when they are five years old, but the males do not become sexually mature until they are six or seven. The pups feed and migrate alone their first year, but after that they join the adult seals for the yearly migration.

The females mate immediately after weaning their pups, and the blastocyst is held in suspension for about three and a half months before implanting and developing into a normal pregnancy. Harp seal pups are born exactly twelve months apart, the timing coinciding with when the arctic ice is thickest.

During the eight-month pregnancy the female feeds in the northern summer feeding grounds, building up the blubber reserves she will need to sustain herself and her pup. Because she fasts while she is nursing, she

© Fred Breummer/Peter Arnold, Inc.

loses nearly 25 percent of her total body weight of 200 pounds (90 kg), some 50 pounds (22.6 kg), at a rate of 6½ pounds (3 kg) per day.

The males have nothing to do with the pups. They wait out the nursing period on ice floes of their own, behaving in a very rowdy and extremely noisy manner. Over fifteen distinct sounds made by adult males have been recorded—a bedlam of grunts, groans, yelps, and squeals. Some of the sounds carry for more than a mile underwater. Harp seals can dive as deep as 600 feet (183 m) and can remain submerged beneath water and ice for up to half an hour.

Toward the end of the two-week nursing period, the males swim over to the whelping ice in groups to see if any of the females are interested yet. When the females are ready, the males compete in magnificent swimming and leaping contests to win their attention. They leap out of the water, turn somersaults, flash by at dazzling speed, and, if that doesn't work, fight and bite, and scratch among themselves. They dive deep, burst from the water in a shower of sparkling droplets, and swim over to make sure the female is watching. At last a female slips into the water to join her mate in a brilliantly acrobatic water ballet. Harp seals mate in the water.

Having mated, the seals return to the sea to feed for two or three weeks before hauling out on the ice in April and May to molt. In pods of twenty to thirty seals they begin the long migration north and east. In the fall of 1760 a French seal hunter watched the harp seal migration pass the northern tip of Newfoundland. He recorded that the harp seals "filled the sea from the landwash seaward to the limit of his vision, and took ten days and ten nights to pass." As recently as 1924, George Allan England wrote of the migration: "They flung up sheaves of foam that flashed in scattered rays of sunshine— swift, joyous forms that plunged, rolled and dived in dashing froth; Nature's supreme last word in vital force and loveliness and grace." The Inuit (Eskimo) call the harp seals *kairulit*, the jumping seal, for the way it leaps from the sea.

In 1844 more than one hundred Newfoundland sealing ships worked a whelping patch that was at least 50 miles (80 km) long and 20 miles (32 km) wide; by conservative estimate, there were more than five million harp seals in that one patch alone. Scientists estimate that there were ten million harp seals before the sealers came. The hunt lasted two hundred years and killed some seventy million harp seals. Today there are two and a half million harp seals.

The transparent white hairs of the pup's coat function as an efficient solar heater. The structure and color of the hair help capture warmth on sunny days, and the fur acts as an insulating blanket to prevent loss of body heat. Skin temperatures as high as 106°F (41°C) have been recorded on days when the air temperature was close to freezing and the pup was lying on ice. The mother in this photo is a young seal. She still sports the spotted coat that precedes the full emergence of the Irish harp pattern that gives harp seals their name.

A Walk on the Ice

All this was background information to my walk on the ice among the Canadian harp seals. There are two other harp seal populations—one in the White Sea off the coast of the Soviet Union and a small group between Jan Mayen and Spitsbergen in the Arctic Sea—but neither is accessible to the wildlife adventurer.

It was a brilliantly sunny day, and the ice glittered. Pups nursed, searching awkwardly for the mother's two small nipples. At my approach the mother seals reared up and uttered a strangely soft warning cry, a gentle effort to defend their babies. Despite their size, they don't seem fierce or frightening at all, but I still steered away from those that made it clear they did not want attention. Instead, I petted and played with the curious, eager pups that wriggled over to see what I was and walked alongside those that squirmed off to look for their mothers when I proved unable to supply either milk or warmth.

Watching the ice carefully for signs of cracking, I made my way from floe to floe. Fine, feathery plumes of snow swirled through the air as sharp, cold gusts of wind caught the edges of icy ridges, 2 and 3 feet (1 m) high. The arctic winds blow this ice world round and round, crunching ice floes together or cracking them apart. Crack lines appear, then fissures, then pressure ridges, which are long windrows of crushed and jumbled ice where two floes have met abruptly. Black frozen afterbirth and thick, little umbilical cords stain the snow-dusted ice. Breathing holes form glistening craters, 1 foot high and 2 or 3 feet (1 m) across. I ate a picnic lunch with our group in the lee of a pressure ridge, wishing desperately that I'd thought to ask for a thermos of hot tea or soup. Cold drinks, lovely as they are, lose much of their appeal in a world of wind and ice. Sitting still, even perched on a thick life-jacket, made my hands and feet ache with cold, so, stuffing my sandwich in my pocket, I wandered off to explore on my own.

Soon I encountered a pup swimming clumsily in a lead, squalling wildly for its mother. She stayed a few feet behind him and let him struggle on his own, while keeping a watchful eye on him. Squawking louder than ever, he reached the edge of the ice, his small flippers hardly sufficient to haul him out and onto the floe. After a series of agonizing slips backward into the water, he finally found a patch of slushy ice that supported him just enough to allow him to scramble out. Wet, cold, and hungry, he headed for the first thing that might be Mom, which happened to be me. A sniff of my boots and gloves was not reassuring; more to the point, it was emphatically not his mother. The small, sodden creature yelped and snapped, catching the finger of my glove in his mouth. For one brief moment he tried sucking it but was soon disappointed. Great tears ran down his face, leaving heart-rending dark streaks along his white muzzle. Still crying piteously, he wriggled off. I walked alongside and stroked his back.

Looking up, I saw his mother observing the entire performance. I petted him one last time, thinking his mother would surely come to him, since he was wailing so industriously. Fully expecting her to haul out onto the ice, I backed away. The pup, suddenly deciding that I was better than nothing, did an abrupt about-face and wriggled after me as fast as his chubby, clumsy little self would go. My heavy Sorel boots proved an insurmountable obstacle. There was no milk there. I have rarely felt as inadequate; I have never been as enchanted. I stroked him until he headed off toward the lead to plead once more for Mom to *please* come feed him. I watched until she came to the edge of the ice and nuzzled his nose, then headed back to the chopper. Even its roaring motor could not break the spell.

A mniotic fluid stains the coat of newborns a bright yellow. The color disappears after a day or two, leaving the pristine white pelage for which harp seal pups are famous.

© Stephen Morello

How To Get There

Air Canada flies from major cities in the United States and Europe to Montreal where you can catch Inter-Canadien to Iles-de-la-Madeleine. Nor-Tours, based at the Chateau Madelinot (P.O. Box 44, Cap-aux-Meules, Iles-de-la-Madeleine, P.Q., Canada GOB 1BO, 418-986-3695), can arrange accommodations, guides, and transportation out to see the seals by helicopter. In the United States, Natural Habitat Wildlife Adventures, Box 789, McAfee, New Jersey 07428 also organizes a Seal Watch tour. (Call (201) 209-4747 in New Jersey, (800) 543-8917 outside New Jersey.) They will arrange transportation on Air Canada and accommodations and provide you with a survival suit to wear on the seal watching tours. Other activities such as seal biologist lectures, wildlife photography seminars, and cross-country skiing are offered as well.

© Steven Morello

VITAL STATISTICS

CLASSIFICATION	DATE OF IDENTIFICATION	POPULATION ESTIMATE	LENGTH/WEIGHT (MALE/FEMALE/PUP)	LONGEVITY	FOOD
TRUE SEALS					
NORTHERN PHOCIDS					
Baikal Seal	1788	50,000	4 ft. (1.3 m) 187 lbs. (85 kg) 4 ft. (1.3 m) 187 lbs. (85 kg) 28 inches (70 cm) 6.5 lbs. (3 kg)	*	various fish
Bearded Seal	1777	500,000	7.4 ft. (2.5 m) 550 lbs. (250 kg) 7.4 ft. (2.5 m) 550 lbs. (250 kg) 4.3 ft. (1.3 m) 66-88 lbs. (30-40 kg)	31 years	flounder, sculpin, polar cod, crabs, shrimp
Caspian Seal	1788	600,000	5 ft. (1.5 m) 190 lbs. (86 kg) 5 ft. (1.5 m) 190 lbs. (86 kg) 28 inches (70 cm) 11 lbs. (5 kg)	*	crustaceans, sprats, spiny sculpin, herring, gobies
Grey Seal	1791	82,000	7.3 ft. (2.2 m) 484 lbs. (220 kg) 6 ft. (1.8 m) 330 lbs. (150 kg) 30 inches (76 cm) 31 lbs. (14 kg)	46 years	various fish, crabs, shrimp
Harbor Seals					
Eastern Atlantic Harbor Seal	1758	50,000	4-6 ft. (1.5-1.8 m) 250 lbs. (113 kg) 3-5 ft (1.2-1.5 m) 250 lbs. (113 kg) * *	35 years	flounder, sole, herring, eel, shellfish (crabs, mussels), squid
Insular Seal	1902	*	5.6-6 ft. (1.7-1.85 m) 130-160 lbs. (59-73 kg) 4-5.6 ft. (1.6-1.70 m) 130-160 lbs. (59-73 kg) 39 inches (98 cm) *	35 years	*
Pacific Harbor Seal	1864	300,000	5.5 ft. (1.62 m) 161 lbs. (73 kg) 5 ft. (1.5 m) 130 lbs. (59 kg) * 53 lbs. (24 kg)	35 years	squid, eels, salmon
Western Atlantic Harbor Seal	1842	12,700	4-6 ft. (1.5-1.8 m) 250 lbs. (113 kg) 3-5 ft. (1.2-1.5 m) 250 lbs. (113 kg) 30 inches (98 cm) 22 lbs. (10 kg)	35 years	herring, flounder, other local fish
Harp Seal	1777	2,500,000	5.3 ft. (1.6 m) 200 lbs. (136 kg) 5.3 ft. (1.6 m) 200 lbs. (136 kg) 35 inches (90 cm) 13-22 lbs. (6-10 kg)	35 years	herring, copelin, cod, shrimp
Hooded Seal	1777	365,000	8.6 ft. (3.6 m) 660 lbs. (300 kg) 6.6 ft. (2 m) 350 lbs. (160 kg) 3.3 ft. (1 m) 33 lbs. (15 kg)	30 years	squid, cod, halibut
Larga Seal	1811	400,000	5.3-5.6 ft. (1.6-1.7 m) * 4.6-5.3 ft. (1.4-1.6 m) * 34 inches (85 cm) *	*	*
Northern Elephant Seal	1820	100,000	15 ft. (4.6 m) 6,000 lbs. (2.727 metric tons) 11 ft. (3.4 m) 1,700 lbs. (773 kg) 39 inches (1.0 m) 88 lbs. (40 kg)	20 years	squid, fish, octopus
Ribbon Seal	1783	240,000	5 ft. (1.5 m) 198 lbs. (90 kg) 5 ft. (1.5 m) 198 lbs. (90 kg) 35 inches (90 cm) 23 lbs. (10.5 kg)	20-30 years	arctic cod, pollack, eelpout, shrimp, crab
Ringed Seal	1775	6,500,000	5 ft. (1.5 m) 150 lbs. (68 kg) 5 ft. (1.5 m) 150 lbs. (68 kg) 26 inches (65 cm) 10 lbs. (4.5 kg)	43 years	various fish, shrimp

* Much is still to be learned about the seals of the world. The information here is as yet unknown.

BASIC BIOLOGY

BREEDING AGE (MALE/FEMALE)	MATING SEASON	PRE-PREGNANCY	PREGNANCY	PUPS BORN	NURSING	ADULT MOLTING
8 years 6 years	May–June	*	*	mid-March	2 months	May–June
6 years 5 years	May	2 months	9 months	March–May	2 weeks	March–June
6–7 years *	early March	*	*	late January	2 months	early March
8 years 4–5 years	September–March	3½ months	8 months	September–March	3 weeks	February–March
6 years 3–4 years	late September	3 months	9 months	late June–early July	4–6 weeks	mid-Aug–mid-September
*	April–June	*	*	*	4 weeks	*
5 years 3 years	February–July (varies by latitude)	2 months	9 months	February–July (depending on region)	6 weeks	*
6 years 3–4 years	mid-June	3 months	9 months	mid-May–mid-June (south) mid-June–early July (arctic)	3–4 weeks	July
6–7 years 5 years	mid-March–early April	4½ months	7 months	early March	12 days	April–May
* 3 years	February	3½–4 months	8½ months	late March	4 days	July–August
*	March–May (varies by latitude)	*	*	early February–early May (depending on region)	4 weeks	*
5–7 years 3–6 years	December–February	4 months	8 months	January	1 month	May–July
5 years 4 years	early May	*	*	April–May	1 month	March–July
7 years 5 years	mid-April	3 months	9 months	March–April	2 months	June

V I T A L   S T A T I S T I C S

CLASSIFICATION	DATE OF IDENTIFICATION	POPULATION ESTIMATE	LENGTH/WEIGHT (MALE/FEMALE/PUP)	LONGEVITY	FOOD
SOUTHERN PHOCIDS					
Crabeater Seal	1842	50,000,000	8.6 ft. (2.6 m) 495 lbs. (225 kg) 8.6 ft. (2.6 m) 495 lbs. (225 kg) 5 ft. (1.5 m) *	29 years	krill
Hawaiian Monk Seal	1905	700	7 ft. (2.1 m) 380 lbs. (173 kg) 7.6 ft. (2.3 m) 600 lbs. (273 kg) 3.3 ft. (1 m) 35 lbs. (16 kg)	20 years	eels, octopus, reef fish
Leopard Seal	1820	800,000	10 ft. (3 m) 594 lbs. (270 kg) 12 ft. (3.6 m) * 5 ft. (1.5 m) 66 lbs. (30 kg)	26 years	penguins, squid, octopus, krill, various fish
Mediterranean Monk Seal	1779	1,000	9.25 ft. (2.8 m) 770–880 lbs. (350–400 kg) 9.25 ft. (2.8 m) 770–880 lbs. (350–400 kg) 32 inches (80 cm) 44 lbs. (20 kg)	*	fish, octopus
Ross Seal	1844	150,000	10 ft. (3 m) 440 lbs. (200–210 kg) 8.25 ft. (2.5 m) 440 lbs. (200–210 kg) 38 inches (96 cm) 37.5 lbs. (17 kg)	21 years	octopus, squid, various fish, krill
Southern Elephant Seal	1758	700,000	13.2–16.5 ft. (4.5 m) 7,200 lbs. (3.24 metric tons) 6.6–10 ft. (2–3 m) 1,980 lbs. (900 kg) 39 inches (1.2 m) 88 lbs. (40 kg)	20 years	various fish, octopus, squid
Weddell Seal	1826	500,000	7.4 ft. (2.5 m) 904 lbs. (411 kg) 7.5 ft. (2.6 m) 904 lbs. (411 kg) 4–4.3 ft. (1.2–1.3 m) 66–88 lbs. (30–40 kg)	18 years	various fish, shrimp, squid
West Indian Monk Seal	1850	extinct	8 ft. (2.4 m) * 8 ft. (2.4 m) * * *	*	*

E A R E D   S E A L S

CLASSIFICATION	DATE OF IDENTIFICATION	POPULATION ESTIMATE	LENGTH/WEIGHT (MALE/FEMALE/PUP)	LONGEVITY	FOOD
SEA LIONS					
Australian Sea Lion	1816	5,000	6.6–8.25 ft. (2–2.5 m) 660 lbs. (300 kg) 5.6–6 ft. (1.7–1.8 m) 176 lbs. (80 kg) 28 inches (70 cm) 15.5 lbs. (7 kg)	12 years	various fish, squid, netted sharks
California Sea Lion	1828	99,000	8 ft. (2.4 m) 660 lbs. (300 kg) 6 ft. (1.8 m) 220 lbs. (100 kg) 30 inches (75 cm) 13 lbs. (6 kg)	30 years	squid, octopus, wake, herring, anchovies, eels
Hooker's Sea Lion	1844	6,000	6.6–8.25 ft. (2–2.5 m) * 5.3–6.6 ft. (1.6–2 m) * 30–32 inches (75–80 cm) *	*	penguins, squid, crab, shrimp, crayfish, stones
Southern Sea Lion	1820	240,000	7.6 ft. (2.3 m) 660 lbs. (300 kg) 6 ft. (1.8 m) 317 lbs. (144 kg) 34 inches (75 cm) *	17 years	squid, crustaceans, magellanic penguins, South American fur seals
Steller's Sea Lion	1776	300,000	10 ft. (3 m) 2,000 lbs. (0.9 metric tons) 7.3 ft. (2.2 m) 594 lbs. (270 kg) 3.3 ft. (1 m) 40–48 lbs. (18–22 kg)	17 years	squid, herring, halibut, flounder, cod, salmon
FUR SEALS					
Antarctic Fur Seal	1875	400,000	6 ft. (1.8 m) 308 lbs. (140 kg) 4.3 ft. (1.3 m) 110 lbs. (50 kg) 26 inches (65 cm) 13 lbs. (6 ka)	*	krill, fish, squid

* Much is still to be learned about the seals of the world. The information here is as yet unknown.

BASIC BIOLOGY

BREEDING AGE (MALE/FEMALE)	MATING SEASON	PRE-PREGNANCY	PREGNANCY	PUPS BORN	NURSING	ADULT MOLTING
3-6 years 3½ years	October	*	*	September-October	4 weeks	January
*	April-November	*	*	December-late May	6 weeks	June
3-6 years 5 years	October-January	3 months	8 months	September-January	4 weeks	January-June
*	August	*	*	September-October	6 weeks	*
*	December	2½-3 months	8½-9 months	mid-November	*	January
5-7 years 3-6 years	mid-late October	4 months	7 months	October	3 weeks	December-March (antarctic summer)
* 3 years	December	*	*	late October	6-7 weeks	December-March (antarctic summer)
*	*	*	*	December	*	*
*	October-January	*	*	October-January	1 year	*
9 years 6-8 years	June (California) September-October (Galapagos Islands)	2-3 months	9-10 months	June (California) September-October (Galapagos Islands)	1 year	*
*	February	*	*	*	1 year	late February
6 years 5 years	January	*	*	late December-early January	1 year	April-August
3-8 years 5 years	late August	3-5 months	8 months	mid-June	1-3 years	*
4 years 3-4 years	late December	*	*	December	4 months	*

VITAL STATISTICS

CLASSIFICATION	DATE OF IDENTIFICATION	POPULATION ESTIMATE	LENGTH/WEIGHT (MALE/FEMALE/PUP)	LONGEVITY	FOOD
Cape Fur Seal/ Australian Fur Seal	1776/ 1925	25,000	7.6 ft. (2.3 m) 480-770 lbs. (200-350 kg) 6 ft. (1.9 m) 264 lbs. (120 kg) 25 inches (65 cm) 13 lbs. (6 kg)	20 years/ 16 years	fish, squid, octopus, rock lobster, stones
Galapagos Fur Seal	1904	2,500	5 ft. (1.5 m) * * * * *	*	various fish
Guadalupe Fur Seal	1897	1,000	6 ft. (1.8 m) 299 lbs. (136 kg) * * * *	*	*
Juan Fernandez Fur Seal	1866	800	6.6 ft. (2 m) 350 lbs. (159 kg) * * * *	*	*
New Zealand Fur Seal	1828	40,000	6.6 ft. (2 m) 440 lbs. (200 kg) 5 ft. (1.5 m) 198 lbs. (90 kg) 25 inches (65 cm) 7.7 lbs. (3.5 kg)	*	squid, rock lobster, octopus, penguins
Northern Fur Seal	1758	1,700,000	7 ft. (2.1 m) 400-598 lbs. (182-272 kg) 5 ft. (1.5 m) 95-110 lbs. (43-50 kg) 26 inches (65 cm) 10 lbs. (4.5 kg)	21 years	herring, squid, pollack, cod, eels
South American Fur Seal	1783	320,000	6.3 ft. (1.9 m) 350 lbs. (159 kg) 4.6 ft. (1.4 m) 110 lbs. (50 kg) * 13 lbs. (6 kg)	*	squid, shrimp, sea snails, various fish
Subantarctic Fur Seal	1872	214,000	6 ft. (1.8 m) 308 lbs. (140 kg) 4.3 ft. (1.3 m) 110 lbs. (50 kg) * *	*	squid, krill, fish, rockhopper penguins

THE WALRUS

CLASSIFICATION	DATE OF IDENTIFICATION	POPULATION ESTIMATE	LENGTH/WEIGHT (MALE/FEMALE/PUP)	LONGEVITY	FOOD
North Atlantic Walrus	1758	5,000	9.9 ft. (3 m) 2,640 lbs. (1.2 metric tons) 8.25 ft. (2.5 m) 1,760 lbs. (800 kg) 4 ft. (1.2 m) 132 lbs. (60 kg)	*	clams, cockles, whelks, mussels
North Pacific Walrus	1815	25,000	10.6 ft. (3.2 m) 2,673 lbs. (1.215 metric tons) 8.6 ft. (2.6 m) 891 lbs. (405 kg) 4 ft. (1.2 m) 130 lbs. (63 kg)	40 years	clams, cockles, whelks, octopus, shrimp

* Much is still to be learned about the seals of the world. The information here is as yet unknown.

BASIC BIOLOGY

BREEDING AGE (MALE/FEMALE)	MATING SEASON	PRE-PREGNANCY	PREGNANCY	PUPS BORN	NURSING	ADULT MOLTING
4 years 4 years	December	4 months	7¾ months	November–December	1–2 years	December–January
*	*	*	*	August	*	*
*	May	*	*	June	*	*
*	*	*	*	December	*	*
*	October	*	*	January	1 year	*
8 years	late June	4 months	7¾ months	June–July	3 months	mid-August
*	December	4 months	7¾ months	November	1 year	*
*	December	*	*	late November–late February	10–11 months	January
13–15 years 5–6 years	February	4–5 months	15 months	April–June	2 years	June–July
13–15 years 5–6 years	January–March	4 months	15–16 months	mid-April–mid-June	2–3 years	June–July

SOURCES

Environmental and Conservation Groups

Association for the Protection of Fur
    Bearing Animals
2235 Commercial Drive
Vancouver, British Columbia V5N 4B6

Earth Island Institute
300 Broadway, Suite 28
San Francisco, CA 94133

Environmental Defense Fund
257 Park Avenue South
New York, New York 10010

Environmental Policy Institute
218 D Street, S.E.
Washington, D.C. 20003

Friends of the Earth
377 City Road
London, EC1
England

Greenpeace
Fort Mason Center
Building E
San Francisco, CA 94123

Greenpeace
30 Islington Green
London, N1
England

International Fund for Animal Welfare
275 Mill Way/P.O. Box 212
Barnstable, Massachusetts 02630

Marine Mammal Fund
Fort Mason Center
Building E
San Francisco, CA 94123

National Wildlife Federation
1326 Massachusetts Avenue, N.W.
Mailing Address: 1412 16th Street
Washington, D.C. 20036

Oceanic Society
Building E-225
Fort Mason Center
San Francisco, CA 94123

    National Headquarters:
    1536 16th Street N.W.
    Washington, D.C., 20036

World Wildlife Fund UK
Panda House
Wayside Park
Godalming
Surrey, GU7 1XR
England

Government Agencies

Environmental Protection Agency
Enforcement and Compliance Monitoring
401 M Street, S.W.
Washington, D.C. 20460

House Merchant Marine and Fisheries
    Committee
Subcommittee on Fisheries, Wildlife
    Conservation, and the Environment
543 HOB Annex 2
Washington, D.C. 20515

Ministry of Agriculture, Fisheries, and Food
Whitehall Place
London, SW1
England

National Oceanic and Atmospheric
    Administration (NOAA)
Commerce Department
14th Street & Constitution Avenue N.W.
Washington, D.C. 20230

National Marine Fisheries Service
1825 Connecticut Avenue, N.W.
Washington, D.C. 20235

Research Centers

California Academy of Sciences
Steinhardt Aquarium
Golden Gate Park
San Francisco, CA 94118

California Marine Mammal Center
Fort Cronkhite
Marine Headlands
Golden Gate National Recreation Area
Sausalito, CA 94965

University of California, Santa Cruz
Biology Department
Santa Cruz, CA
Attn: Dr. Burney LeBoeuf

BIBLIOGRAPHY

Breummer, Fred. *The Life of the Harp Seal.* Montreal: Optimum Publishing, 1977.

Breummer, Fred. *Season of the Seal.* Minocqua, Wisconsin: North Word Press, 1988.

Cousteau, Jacques-Yves and Phillippe Diole (Translated from the French by J.F. Bernard). *Diving Companions: Sea Lion–Elephant Seal–Walrus.* New York: Doubleday, 1974.

Daugherty, Anita. *Marine Mammals of California* (UCSMGAP85-3). University of California Sea Grant Marine Advisory Program, 1985.

Davies, Brian. *Savage Luxury.* New York: Ballantine Books, 1970.

De Santis, Marie. *California Currents.* Novato, CA: Presidio Press, 1985.

Durrell, Gerald. *The Whispering Land.* Middlesex: Penguin Books, 1961.

FAO Advisory Committee on Marine Resources Research, Food and Agriculture Organization of the United Nations, Working Party on Marine Mammals. *Mammals in the Seas (Vol. 1).* Rome, 1978.

Fay, Francis. *Ecology and Biology of the Pacific Walrus, Odobenus Rosmarus Divergens Illiger* (North American Fauna Number 74). Washington, D.C.: United States Department of the Interior, 1982.

King, Judith. *Seals of the World* (2nd. ed.). New York: Cornell University Press, 1983.

Lavigne, David and Kit Kovacs. *Harps & Hoods: Ice-breeding Seals of the Northwest Atlantic.* Waterloo, Canada: University of Waterloo Press, 1988.

LeBoeuf, Burney, and Stephanie Kaza (Eds.). *The Natural History of Ano Nuevo.* Pacific Grove, CA: The Boxwood Press, 1981.

Miles, Hugh and Mike Salisbury. *Kingdom of the Ice Bear: A Portrait of the Arctic.* British Broadcasting Corporation: London, 1985.

Mowat, Farley. *Sea of Slaughter.* Toronto and London: Bantam Books, 1986.

O'Neill, Catherine and Judith Rinard. *Amazing Animals of the Sea: Marine Mammals.* National Geographic Society, 1981.

Orr, Robert. *Marine Mammals of California.* Berkeley and London: University of California, 1972.

Ridgeway, S.H. and R.J. Harrison (Eds.), *Handbook of Marine Mammals (Vol. 1 & 2) The Walrus, Sea Lions, Fur Seals, and the Sea Otter* (vol. 1); *Seals* (vol. 2). London: Academic Press, 1981.

Ronald, K., L.M. Hanley, P.J. Healy, and L.J. Selley. *An Annotated Bibliography on the Pinnipeda.* Charlottenlund: International Council for the Exploration of the Sea, 1976.

INDEX

ADDITIONAL CREDITS